BREAD BLESSED AND BROKEN

Eucharistic Prayers and Fraction Rites

Edited by
John P. Mossi, S.J.

PAULIST PRESS
New York / Paramus / Toronto

Library of Congress Catalog Card Number: 74-16844

ISBN: 0-8091-1855-6

Published by Paulist Press
Editorial Office: 1865 Broadway, N.Y., N.Y. 10023
Business Office: 400 Sette Drive, Paramus, N.J. 07652

Printed and bound in the United States of America

CONTENTS

In memory of
Joe Wall, S.J.
and
Ed Hagemann, S.J.

With gratitude for their
celebration and love
of life.

Introduction

The liturgical movement, now over one hundred and fifty years old, is moving into a new phase. We have built upon the important and sensitive work of the nineteenth century monastic liturgists in their recovery of our liturgical tradition. We are now reaping the benefits in our own century of the transmission of this tradition to the clergy and people. Our Sunday and weekday liturgies are the concrete, pastoral application of this tradition. All of this past study, research, struggle for updating, and theological searching reached its watershed in the *Constitution on the Sacred Liturgy* of the Second Vatican Council. The privilege is ours to witness this great revival of Christian worship. We are the inheritors of a liturgical reconstruction based on the principle of the restoration of the liturgy of the primitive Church with the necessary pastoral adaptations for the contemporary worshipper.

But just as the Vatican Council was the culminating point for all the liturgical endeavors that went before, it was also the stepping stone to what was and is to come after. The document on the liturgy contains within itself a number of suggested paths for the liturgy of the post-Vatican era. These refer not so much to new rites as to a different operating principle. It is now not a question of restoration, but of creativity, not pastoral application of an older liturgy but the discovery of new services in the faith community's experimental dialogue with its culture. It is now not so much a matter of more changes in our rites as it is worshipping in a new perspective. Multiple and distinct liturgical services will emerge because the horizons of the Christian community have changed.

Our liturgical reforms up to the present time have been mainly concerned with suppressing the irrelevant, reviving older liturgical forms, adding what is considered to be pastorally helpful, and making adaptations in light of our culture. This approach was primarily concerned to emphasize our continuity with the past. But what we really need now is that kind of reform which places a stress on discontinuity with what has gone before.

The liturgical reforms of the future must be characterized more by transformation than restoration. The reason that a transformative process is required is that liturgy is no longer confined to and reflective of a well-defined Catholic community. Liturgy has a wider reference to life as human in the world. This implies greater discontinuity with our Catholic tradition than was previously the case.

Since most of the present rites were molded by a theology which viewed sacramental presence in terms of a well-defined church, they are still unable to relate their communal words and actions to the fundamental symbolic nature of creation. We are now more sensitive to the fact that the holy can be brought to visibility through each creature itself. To be an authentic human being is to be the manifestation of the sacred. It is precisely the holy as found in all of human life that must be thematized and concretized in the Christian sacramental encounter. But when this presence of the sacred in human existence is ambiguous or even completely hidden, religious symbols such as sacraments communicate little or nothing. Liturgy is that which celebrates, and therefore presupposes, the growth of man toward his true humanity, toward becoming more fully a symbol of God's love in his ordinary living.

Specifically, this means that the liturgical community must realize itself as a sign witnessing to the salvific value of the humanization process. The eucharist as the chief expression of this community as community is not a sign for an isolated assembly. It is the recognition that the human is the primary symbol of God's redemptive love. The eucharistic rite cannot become a countersign of separateness because all mankind is called to unification. We have too long stressed the elements of the eucharistic meal over the meal itself. A recovery of the meal aspect of the eucharistic liturgy will enable it to be more clearly the paradigm of the fact that all forms of human brotherhood and bodily sharing are forces for union with God.

Concretely, the implications of transformational reform are:
(1) We must examine in greater detail the ritual structures that support the central symbolic actions of worship.
(2) The liturgy will always have structural problems. The solution to these problems is discovered in the way in which we employ the structures.
(3) Liturgy is its own catechesis. Symbols that need explanation are deficient.
(4) We must reevaluate our symbols and use those which will reach people more fully in worship.
(5) We should not ask the liturgy to do for us what we are able to do for ourselves and for our brothers and sisters in the world.

It is for these reasons that new Eucharistic Prayers are needed. Their language, imagery, poetry, and expressions should be able to facilitate the resounding doxology of today's person of faith. Moreover, the ritual action of the breaking of bread, real bread, of course, should be restored to the liturgy since it has a meaning fundamental for the life of the Church today. It recalls the story of how the early Christians recognized the Lord's presence in the very human context of a meal. The breaking and participation in the one bread was seen in the Corinthian Church as a healing remedy to the differences and divisions among them. A restoration of this rite to the consciousness of Christians will hopefully proclaim that reconciliation is one of the chief ex-emplifications of becoming more fully human. I believe that Father John P. Mossi, S.J. has made an important contribution to the transformative process of liturgical reform by offering this collection of Eucharistic Prayers and Fraction Rites.

JAMES L. EMPEREUR, S.J.
*Jesuit School of Theology
at Berkeley*

Preface

We can all probably remember those incense-filled days when the mark of liturgical excellence was a strict adherence to the rubrics of the *Missale Romanum*. Nowadays liturgical excellence demands a new dwelling place, a home in the prayerful hearts and creativity of the People of God. Liturgical books, this one included, are, at best, skeletal. They challenge people to embody in action what they read. Only a dedicated people, filled with the love of God, can consistently create celebrations with substance and meaning. They must be willing to meditate on the events of the Testaments, work on worship committees, and give to the liturgy the attention and talent that is its due.

Liturgical planners know that the task of reverently executing the liturgy is both exhausting and time consuming. Constant attention must be given to all aspects of the liturgy: the homily, prayers, and music, as well as the participation of the congregation, the liturgical furnishings, the presidential qualities of the celebrant, the sign value of the liturgical actions, the presence of women, lectors, lay deacons, and special communion ministers, the type of vestments worn, the use of media, and on and on. Gone are the days of the solo celebration. Such attempts are guaranteed cul-de-sacs. The basic ingredients of good celebration require a consultation with experts, a familiarity with available liturgical resources, and a sensitivity to the arts.

The liturgical confusion of the past years has destroyed some of the valuable elements in the old liturgy. But from these ashes a liturgical renaissance is beginning to blossom. Presently we are engaged in the exciting process of rediscovering the significance of liturgy, and perhaps learning for the first time how to celebrate.

As a contribution to the liturgical resurgence of which we are all part, this book attempts to respond to the ever-increasing demands for thematic eucharistic prayers and fraction prayers to accompany the breaking of the bread. These special prayers are models, outlines, patterns that of necessity have to be adapted to the needs of each community. Such adaptations will enrich these prayers with the charism of the local church.

In compiling this book, I am acutely aware of my indebtedness to many people, especially James Empereur, S.J., Michael Moynahan, S.J., and my brother Jesuits from Berkeley whose prayerful spirit fills these pages. May their songs of praise likewise inspire you.

JOHN P. MOSSI, S.J.
Feast of the Risen Lord, 1974

PART I: BREAD BLESSED

The Eucharistic Prayer

The Christian Church is indebted to the tradition of the Jews for the basic structure of the eucharistic prayer. The Great Thanksgiving, as the eucharistic prayer is commonly called, is really a descendant of the berakah, an Old Testament prayer of blessing that is integral to the Passover Meal. It is within the religious setting of the Pasch that Jesus, faithful to his religious training and the Jewish customs of the time, celebrated the Last Supper. He gave thanks over the bread, and then, at the end of the meal, over the wine. In effect, Jesus prayed the blessing of the berakah praising his Father for his constant love and mercy.

An examination of the form of the berakah reveals five characteristic elements which have influenced the structure of the eucharistic prayer. These elements of the berakah are: (1) the prayer is addressed to the Lord Yahweh; (2) it is a joyful proclamation of praise and thanksgiving; (3) the prayer remembers God's many saving acts performed throughout history for his people; (4) it asks God to continue to bless his people and to remain faithful to his covenants; (5) the berakah concludes with a doxology, a closing hymn of praise.

When the early Christians, many of whom were Jews, gathered to celebrate the eucharist, they followed the berakah pattern of prayer incorporating the Lord's institutional narrative over the bread and wine in the context of the paschal mystery. True to the style of the berakah, the early eucharistic prayers were spontaneous. In the words of St. Justin, the celebrant "gave thanks, as he was able." Even though these eucharistic prayers were improvised, the celebrant followed a fixed order in praying the thanksgiving. In this manner the primitive Church ably blended spontaneous and creative expression with a definite structure.

By the third century, written outlines of eucharistic prayers were common. One such outline is the canon of St. Hippolytus of Rome which is the model for the present day Eucharistic Prayer II. Its brevity is rather deceptive because at the appropriate places the celebrant would embellish the thanksgiving prayer with certain thematic improvisations. Gradually, the eucharistic prayer texts became fixed.

As the main churches of Rome, Antioch, and Alexandria increased in size and influence, their eucharistic liturgies reflected more their respective geographical and theological traditions. In the Western Church, the main elements of the Roman Canon were established by the seventh century. Because the Roman Canon was compiled from Gallic, Celtic, and old Roman liturgies, it lacked the inherent unity typical of the Oriental Anaphoras. The prayer became further cluttered with such secondary elements as the "Holy, Holy," intercessory prayers for the Pope, the living and the dead, and the commemoration of local Roman saints and martyrs.

As the ecclesial power of Rome grew, so did its control of the liturgy. By the twelfth century, the Roman Canon was the only eucharistic prayer used in the celebrations of the Roman Rite. The reforms of the Council of Trent as well as the publication of the *Missale Romanum* in 1570 by Pope Pius V confirmed and strengthened the privileged position of the Roman Canon.

Further eucharistic developments had to wait patiently for the spirit of the Second Vatican Council to renew and broaden the worship of the Church. In addition to a general reform of the liturgy that included the revision of all liturgical books, the use of the vernacular, and the power of Conferences of Bishops to determine local liturgical adaptations, three new eucharistic prayers were created. Eucharistic Prayers II, III, and IV corrected the deficiencies of the present Eucharistic Prayer I. They clearly emphasized the paschal mystery of the Lord and avoided the unnecessary repetitions and lack of order found in the Roman Canon.

The revised *General Instruction* which accompanies the new *Roman Missal*, 1974, enumerates in section 55 the chief components of these eucharistic prayers in the following way:

(a) *Thanksgiving* (expressed especially in the preface): in the name of the entire people of God, the priest praises the Father and gives him thanks for the work of salvation or for some special aspect of it in keeping with the day, feast, or season.

(b) *Acclamation*: united with the angels, the congregation sings or recites the *Sanctus*. This acclamation forms part of the eucharistic prayer, and all the people join with the priest in singing or reciting it.

(c) *Epiclesis*: in special invocations the Church calls on God's power and asks that the gifts offered by men may be consecrated, that is, become the body and blood of Christ, and that the victim may become a source of salvation for those who are to share in communion.

(d) *Narrative of the institution and consecration*: in the words and actions of Christ, the sacrifice he instituted at the Last Supper is celebrated, when under the appearances of bread and wine he offered his body and blood, gave them to his Apostles to eat and drink, and commanded them to carry on this mystery.

(e) *Anamnesis*: in fulfillment of the command received from Christ through the Apostles, the Church keeps his memorial by recalling especially his passion, resurrection, and ascension.

(f) *Offering*: in this memorial, the Church—and in particular the Church here and now assembled—offers the victim to the Father in the Holy Spirit. The Church's intention is that the faithful not only offer the spotless victim but also learn to offer themselves and daily to be drawn into ever more perfect union, through Christ the Mediator, with the Father and with each other, so that at last God may be all in all.

(g) *Intercessions*: the intercessions make it clear that the eucharist is celebrated in communion with the whole Church of heaven and earth, and that the offering is made for the Church and all its members, living and dead, who are called to share in the salvation and redemption acquired by the body and blood of Christ.

(h) *Final doxology*: the praise of God is expressed in the doxology which is confirmed and concluded by the acclamation of the people.

Keeping in mind the spirit of the primitive Church, the liturgical thrusts of recent years, and the guidelines of the *Instruction*, the eucharistic prayers of this book faithfully retain the general patterns traditional to the eucharistic prayer. These thanksgiving prayers are highly thematic, blending Old and New Testament personages and events. They are rich in their praise and blessing of the Father. They have the advantage of being originally written in English and thus possess a native cadence and flow.

Special attention should be paid to the position of the eucharistic acclamation, the epiclesis, and the intercessions in each of these eucharistic prayers. The eucharistic acclamation of the assembly has been repositioned after the anamnesis to allow the paschal mystery of Christ's dying and rising to be proclaimed first by the celebrant. The epiclesis, the prayer in which we ask the Holy Spirit to help us achieve the unity celebrated in the

Lord's meal, then follows the eucharistic acclamation. This sequence of thematic praise, remembrance, and petition permits a smooth flow in the eucharistic structure. In the majority of the prayers, the number of intercessions is reduced in the hope that the various prayers for the living and the dead will be handled in the General Intercessions. Regarding the layout of the eucharistic prayers, each prayer is divided into stanzas to facilitate proclamation and use at concelebration.

Hopefully these models of eucharistic prayers will begin to meet the growing liturgical need for canons which capture and reflect the spirit of particular occasions.

Eucharistic Prayers

1. CREATIVITY

We give you thanks and praise, Father,
for a universe beautiful beyond belief,
for a world of possibilities beyond dreams.

We praise you for things,
rocks and trees, lakes and fields,
plants and stars.
And we praise you for people
who come into our lives
and challenge us to grow
and to become more fully human.

We praise you for our imaginations,
for the ability to dream
and conceive of a world in harmony singing your
    praises.

We sing out to you our thanks and praise, Father,
because you are a God of creativity.
With all your wondrous works
we now joyfully proclaim the words of your prophet
    Isaiah:

Holy, holy, holy Lord . . .

We praise you, loving Father,
that you are a God of dreamers and of visionaries.
You allowed Noah to dream of a world at peace with
      you,
and his dream was fulfilled.
You gave Abraham a vision of a new people,
numerous as the stars of heaven,
and a nation was formed.
Moses and his people dreamed of freedom,
and you led them to a land flowing with milk and
      honey.
Through the ages, people have dreamed of seeing
      you,
and you kept your promise fully
by giving us your Son, Jesus.

We sing your praises, God our Father,
because of the hope we have been given by your
      Word, Jesus.
Speaking your wisdom, he has told us
that we are your children
destined one day to see you face to face
and live with you in the kingdom of heaven.
He has called us blessed
if only we be poor in spirit,
peacemakers, seekers after justice,
and merciful toward all people.

We praise you, loving Father,
because Jesus has given us the Spirit
that we might dream dreams
and experience a new hope
in the fullness of life and love.

We now remember that night when
Jesus shared his vision
giving us proof of his abiding love for us.
While he was at supper with his friends,
he took bread, broke it,
and gave it to them after the blessing, saying:
Share this bread among you.
This is my body, broken for you.

After the meal, he said another blessing
over a cup of wine:
Drink from this cup, all of you.
This is the new covenant in my blood,
poured out for the forgiveness of sins.
Whenever you share this meal,
do it in memory of me.

Father, gathered around this table,
we call to mind the life Jesus lived among us.
We celebrate the death which he accepted
in fidelity to your will and out of love for us.
We remember his victory over death
which has made us men and women free to dream.
We recall that he returned to you
and sent the Holy Spirit
to be our source of strength and courage and vision.
In the spirit of his perfect prayer of love to you,
accept this bread of heaven and cup of salvation.

We give you thanks and praise, Father,
and joyfully proclaim the great mystery of our faith:
    Christ has died,
    Christ is risen,
    Christ will come again.

Help us to be open
that we might receive your Spirit.
May this Holy Spirit be a presence in our lives
and form us into a People of God, a nation of
        believers
who will proclaim to all the world
that everything is possible for those who love you.

We make our prayer through Jesus Christ, your Son.
    Through him,
    with him,
    in him,
    in the unity of the Holy Spirit,
    all glory and honor is yours,
    almighty Father,
    for ever and ever.
    Amen.

Paul Roy, S.J.

2. PRAISE AND THANKSGIVING

Zechariah's berakah prayer as found in Luke 1:68-79 is the
scriptural basis for part of this thanksgiving.

Praise and thanksgiving to you, heavenly Father,
for you are a God of nearness.
You walk in the cool of our earthly garden
and gently call us in the depth of our hearts.

Praise and thanksgiving to you, loving Father,
for providing us with the care and concern
of families and communities, so that we can
all the more experience your creative goodness.

Praise and thanksgiving to you, almighty Father,
for the beauty and mystery that abounds in our
     world,
for tree-filled mountains that touch the blue of sky,
for wine-dark oceans that teem with wonders:
all this so that we may marvel at your creative
     goodness.

We now join all of creation
in the continual shouting of your praise,
and with your holy people everywhere
we raise our voices and joyfully sing:

     Holy, holy, holy Lord . . .

Blessed are you, Father,
because you have visited
and ransomed your people.

You have raised up a horn of saving strength for us
in the house of your servant David,
according to the promise which you made
by the lips of your prophets from the beginning.

Blessed are you, Father,
for you are faithful in your promise of salvation.
You remember your holy covenant.

You swore an oath to our father Abraham,
enabling us to live without fear in your service,
delivering us from the hands of our enemies,
and permitting us to spend our days in the holiness of
        your sight.

Blessed are you, Father,
for the many servants of your word
who proclaim to the people
the good news of freedom from the bondage of sin.

You sent your Son to be our brother.
He is our long awaited dawn
and light to our hearts.
He guides us along the way of peace.

Blessed are you, Father,
that your Son has given us a meal
to celebrate your many saving acts.
While at table
Jesus took bread
and praised your steadfast mercy.
Then he broke the bread
and gave it to his friends with the words:
Take this, all of you, and eat,
this is my body which is given up for you.

At the end of the meal,
he took the cup of blessing.
He gave you thanks,
and giving the cup to his friends, said:
Take this, all of you, and drink.
This cup is the new covenant in my blood,
shed for you and for all people
so that sins may be forgiven.
Do this in memory of me.

Father, recalling your Son's birth, his living among
        us,
his dying for us, his rising in triumph over death,
his entering into glory, and ever awaiting
his coming at the fullness of time,
we surrender ourselves to you
through this life-giving bread, this cup of blessing.

With great joy, let us proclaim our salvation:
        When we eat this bread and drink this cup,
        we proclaim your death, Lord Jesus,
        until you come in glory.

May we who are nourished by this holy meal
be sanctified by your Holy Spirit
and become a sign of unity and hope for the world.

As we ask you to keep us in your fatherly protection,
we also pray that your law of love and peace guide
        our actions.
May all be freed from the slavery of sin,
hunger, sickness and discrimination.
Grant that nations may experience your justice
and live in the harmony of your unifying Spirit.

As always, we make our prayer
in the name of Jesus.
        Through him,
        with him,
        in him,
        in the unity of the Holy Spirit,
        all glory and honor is yours,
        almighty Father,
        for ever and ever.
        Amen.

John Mossi, S.J.

3. HOPE

Father, we praise you and we bless you.
You have made us and we belong to you.
You do not hide from us. You are not distant.
You have revealed yourself
and your great love for us
in all your wonderful works.

We see you in the strength of mountains,
the solitude of deserts,
and in gentle and refreshing rain.
We see you in the height of skies and ocean depths,
in birds that soar and fish that swim.
We see you in the hope of sunrise,
the relief and rest of sunset.
All your works proclaim your love.

As children, surrounded and protected
by the warmth of a Father's love,
we join all creation in rejoicing, in celebrating
your great care and concern for us.
It is in this spirit, that we raise our voices
and praise your name:

      Holy, holy, holy Lord . . .

Father, we thank you for speaking
your greatest word of love to us: Jesus Christ.
He came to show us clearly who you are.
He taught us how to call you God and Father.

We are your children, your image.
We thank you that when we sinned
you sent us Jesus Christ, our brother,
to free the child in each of us
to grow in your life and spirit.

And of all he said and did,
we thank you for his greatest gift to us.
On the night before he died,
Jesus gathered his friends together for a meal
and shared with them his life and love.
While they were at supper, he took some bread,
gave you thanks, broke it,
and passed it among them saying:
Take this, all of you, and eat.
This is my body given up for you.

Then he took the cup of wine, said the blessing,
and gave it to them saying:
Take this, all of you, and drink.
This is the cup of my blood,
poured out for people everywhere
so sins may be forgiven.
This is a new and everlasting covenant.
Do this in memory of me.

Father, we thank you for Christ's life among us,
the example he has left us
of how to live a life of love.
We gratefully recall his death,

and how he shows us a way
to die to self and live for others.
And finally, we remember the hope we have
in Jesus' resurrection and ascension:
the hope of the seed that falls into the ground,
the hope of the grapes that yield to crushing,
the hope we cling to with childlike tenacity,
the hope of new and fuller life.

Together, now, as a community of believers,
we proclaim the fullness of our faith:
> Christ has died,
> Christ is risen,
> Christ will come again.

Send us your Spirit, Father,
the Spirit Christ has promised us,
so the child in each of us can grow.
Help us rediscover creativity and imagination
and all the ways in which we can be
most like you.

Give us your eyes and restore our vision.
Teach us to find you in the present moment
you have given us.
Help us to seek and find you
where you are to be found
in the ordinary, day to day
living out of our lives.

We make our prayer to you, Father,
in the name of your Son, Jesus,
who is our hope.

Through him,
with him,
in him,
in the unity of the Holy Spirit,
all glory and honor is yours,
almighty Father,
for ever and ever.
Amen.

Michael Moynahan, S.J.

4. ALLELUIA

This Easter Vigil prayer is set to the melody of *Ye Sons and Daughters of the Lord*. Underlined syllables and words receive two notes. The Prayer reflects the principal themes of the vigil readings.

Cel. Alleluia! Alleluia! Alleluia!
Cong. Alleluia! Alleluia! Alleluia!

Creation
Cel. Father of Mercy, Lord of Life
Out of the darkness, you brought light.
From earth and water, you brought life.
Alleluia!
Cong. Alleluia! Alleluia! Alleluia!

Exodus
Cel. From Egypt's slavery you led us forth
Cloud and fire, you went on before
Leading us through the desert waste.
Alleluia!
Cong. Alleluia! Alleluia! Alleluia!

Covenant
Cel. Love is your Covenant, faithful and true
Binding us to one another and you
Promising faithfulness unto your day.
Alleluia!
Cong. Alleluia! Alleluia! Alleluia!

The Land

Cel.   Over the Jordan, a <u>bright</u> new home
        <u>Milk</u> and <u>honey</u> <u>for</u> us flowed
        <u>Fruit</u> and <u>grain</u> your mercy bestowed.
            Alleluia!

Cong. Alleluia! Alleluia! Alleluia!

Exile

Cel.   Back from our <u>exile</u>, home to our land
        <u>Your</u> great <u>mercy</u>, your mighty hand
        Freed us <u>again</u> to live in your love. Alleluia!

Cong. Alleluia! Alleluia! Alleluia!

Jesus

Cel.   Out of our <u>midst</u> you called forth a man
        Speaking your <u>words</u>, proclaiming your day,
        Jesus of Nazareth, Son of your love.
            Alleluia!

Cong. Alleluia! Alleluia! Alleluia!

Death

Cel.   For love of <u>us</u>, he laid down his life
        Showing us clearly how great is your love.
        From his torn <u>heart</u>, our new life is born.
            Alleluia!

Cong. Alleluia! Alleluia! Alleluia!

Bread

Cel.   Before he <u>died</u>, he took up the bread
        Blessed you and broke it and to us he said,
        This is my <u>body</u>, given for you. Alleluia!

Cong.   Alleluia! Alleluia! Alleluia!

Cup

Cel.   Praising your faithfulness, he took the cup.
          This is my blood of the new covenant
          Poured out for <u>you</u> and <u>all</u> mankind. Alleluia!
Cong.   Alleluia! Alleluia! Alleluia!

Resurrection

Cel.   From death's dark <u>hold</u>, your <u>mighty</u> love
          Raised him on high in your <u>Spirit</u>'s pow'r
          Conquering <u>death</u> for<u>ev</u>ermore. Alleluia!
Cong.   Alleluia! Alleluia! Alleluia!

Epiclesis

<small>(extra note)</small>

Cel.   Pour forth on <u>us</u>, your <u>waiting</u> people
          Your Holy <u>Spirit</u>, <u>make</u> us one
          The one true body of Jesus your Son.
              Alleluia!
Cong.   Alleluia! Alleluia! Alleluia!

Doxology

Cel.   Glory and honor and power are yours
          In Jesus Christ and your Spirit of love
          Now and for<u>ev</u>er, <u>praise</u> to you. Alleluia!
Cong.   Alleluia! Alleluia! Alleluia!

Alleluia

Cel. and Cong. Alleluia! Alleluia!
                  Alleluia! Alleluia!
                  Alleluia! Alleluia! Alleluia!

Joseph Powers, S.J.

5.   RESURRECTION

The characteristic sign of the early Christians was their love for one another. This prayer uses the kiss of peace as a paschal proclamation of the mystery of faith.

Heavenly Father,
death and birth become one mystery
in the rising of your Son,
a mystery in which our lives
receive new meaning in your love.
We give you thanks and call upon your name
to bring us to birth
in the power of his death and rising.

We thank you, God our Father,
that you have shown us the power of faith,
the beauty of love in the life of your Son, Jesus
      Christ.
By raising Christ from the dead
you have given us the hope of eternal life
and the call to share that hope with all nations.
May we have the courage to live as fully as Jesus did,
to serve our fellow man with generosity and joy.

We thank you, Father
that you have freed us from the power of sin
and have given us victory over death in your Son,
      Jesus Christ.
May we who have died in baptism with him
and have been raised to new life with him,
be witnesses to our faith in him

so that through us the love of Christ
will be born again into the world.

We thank you, God our Father,
that you have made us your sons and daughters
by raising our brother Jesus from the dead.
May he bless our hearts
with happiness and peace
at this time of Easter joy.

We thank you for this unforgettable man.
He is the fullness of life,
the beginning and the end,
the first born of all your creation,
light of the world,
the first to be born from the dead.
He became the least among us,
bread broken and passed from hand to hand.
He has given us this sign of his love.

On the evening before his suffering and death,
he took bread into his hands,
he blessed you, broke the bread,
and gave it to his disciples with the words:
Take and eat.
This is my body which will be given up for you.

He also took the cup
and giving thanks to you, said:
This cup is the new covenant in my blood
shed for you and for all mankind
so that sins may be forgiven.
Do this in memory of me.

We thank you, Father,
for the death and resurrection of your Son.
He has stretched the horizons of this life to infinity.
As you lifted him up in glory
to reveal to us your love,
lift us up so that we will give ourselves
to one another in the same spirit
that Christ gave himself to us.

Let us proclaim this mystery
by exchanging with one another
the love of Christ:
(The kiss of peace is passed among the assembly.)

Send upon us, Father,
the Spirit of the Risen Christ
that he may enlighten the eyes of our hearts
so that we may witness to your love
until your Son returns in glory.
May his Spirit teach us how to pray
until the day of his return.

Then your name will be made holy on earth,
    through Jesus Christ,
    with him,
    and in him,
    for ever and ever.
    Amen.

James Empereur, S.J.

6. PEACE

We thank you, almighty Father,
because for us you have raised your Son,
our Lord Jesus Christ,
from the dead.

In him you have sent us peace
and freed us from death.
He has become our forgiveness,
our hope, and our life.
Because you raised him
and gave him glory,
we give you thanks
and join your whole creation
in a hymn of praise, saying:

> Holy, holy, holy Lord . . .

We thank you, almighty Father,
because from the very beginning
you promised us peace.
Despite our sins and our guilt
you have worked to unlock our hearts.

We sought after the pagan food of Egypt,
and you led us to a land of milk and honey.
We broke away from your covenant,
and you welcomed us back to fellowship.
We turned away from you to idols,
and you returned us from exile.

Finally we locked ourselves within the Law,
and you sent your only Son
to free us from bondage
with a new covenant of freedom.
He has moved among us
teaching and healing,
and we have known him
in the breaking of the bread.

For we remember how,
on the night before he died,
he took bread and wine,
gave you thanks and praise, and said:
This is my body, broken for you,
and my blood, shed for you and all my people
so that sins may be forgiven.
Whenever you do this,
you will do it in memory of me.

And now, Lord, we remember and celebrate
how your Son climbed the cross,
how he suffered and died to free us,
and how he rose from the dead
so that he might bring us peace
and the gift of the Holy Spirit
as a sign of the glory which awaits us.

Let us proclaim our salvation:
    Dying you destroyed our death,
    rising you restored our life.
    Lord Jesus, come in glory.

Send your Holy Spirit, Lord,
upon these gifts and this meal.
May we share this living bread
and this living cup as a people
freed from unbelief and skepticism,
united with the Church and all Christians
by the peace of the resurrection
in Christ Jesus our Lord.

Through him,
with him,
in him,
in the unity of the Holy Spirit,
all glory and honor is yours,
almighty Father,
for ever and ever.
Amen.

Stephen Kuder, S.J.

7. FULFILLMENT

Certain celebrations demand a short eucharistic prayer. Fr. Gelpi's canons possess a careful blend of articulate theology and poetic expression that is particularly appropriate for such occasions.

We praise and thank you, Father in heaven.
You are a faithful God.
You made all things by the power of your word.
And by the Word-made-flesh
you have brought all things to fulfillment.

You are the Lord of times and of seasons.
With love you tend the vine of your planting.
With a gentle hand you prune it
so that it may bear abundant fruit.

You are the only God, holy and just.
By your law you have instructed us.
You guide us in the way of salvation.

You are a patient God.
By your prophets you lead us.
You encourage us in our weakness.

In you all things find life.
In you all life finds fulfillment.

And so in fulfillment of your word,
we celebrate your glory as we say:

Holy, holy, holy Lord . . .

We praise you and we thank you
for your Son, Jesus Christ.

He is the Word of life who proceeds from your lips.
By the power of his Spirit our hearts are renewed.

He is the true Vine, we are the branches.
From him we draw our life.

He is the Holy One, the Just One.
He is your living covenant of love.

He is Truth, he is Life.
In him we are forgiven.
In him we are healed.

And so we recall that on the night he was betrayed
he took bread into his hands.
He blessed your name.
Then he broke the bread
and gave it to his disciples with the words:
Take this and eat it.
This is my body which will be broken for you.

And after the supper he took a cup of wine.
Again he blessed your name.
Then he gave the cup to his disciples with the words:
Take this and drink from it, all of you.
For this is the cup of my blood,
the blood of the new and everlasting covenant.
It will be poured out for you
and for all for the forgiveness of sins.
Each time you do this,
do it in memory of me.

Father, we are gathered here to renew
this sign of your faithful love.
We remember that Jesus died for us.
But by his death he fulfilled your word.
And by his resurrection he has renewed
the face of the earth.

Transform us, then, by the power of his Spirit.
Re-create our hearts in love.
And bring us and all nations
to the fulfillment of our hopes
in Christ Jesus our Lord.

Through him,
with him,
in him,
in the unity of the Holy Spirit,
all glory and honor is yours,
almighty Father,
for ever and ever.
Amen.

Donald Gelpi, S.J.

8. FAITHFULNESS

Praise to you, Lord God,
for you are a God of power,
the power of faithful love for your people.
You call each of us into being
and desire that we realize your love for us
through our love for one another.

Praise to you, Lord God,
for you spoke to Abraham,
promising that all the families of the earth
would be blessed through him.
Through Abraham you formed a holy people,
a people who would carry on your promise.
You continually spoke to them,
repeating your promise to the children of Abraham
and their descendants through your prophets.

Praise to you, Lord God,
for you kept your promise to us.
In your own time you showed your faithfulness
by sending your Son.

He showed us how to love by his obedience to you.
Aware of your faithfulness,
and striving to imitate that love
which your Son lived,
we praise you in the words of your prophet Isaiah:

Holy, holy, holy Lord . . .

Blessed are you, Lord God,
for your Son Jesus the Christ.
You sent him to rule over your people
with the majesty of your name.
He came from Bethlehem,
from the least of the clans of Judah,
to bring peace to us, your people,
to teach us your name
and to fulfill your promise of blessing to mankind,
a blessing which he accomplished
by giving himself to all men
through obedience to your will.

On the night that he was betrayed,
as a sign of that blessing,
he took some bread and gave you thanks for your
        faithfulness.
He broke the bread, gave it to his friends, and said:
This is my body which is for you.
Do this as a memorial of me.

In the same way, after supper, he took the cup and
        said:
This cup is the fulfillment of the promise in my
        blood.
Whenever you drink it, do this as a memorial of me.

Father, we eat this meal in memory of your Son.
We recall that he suffered and died in obedience to
        your will,

but that you raised him from the dead.
Thus, he became the first man born into eternity.
You have kept your promise to us,
making him a blessing to all people.

Let us proclaim God's everlasting love:
Christ has died,
Christ is risen,
Christ will come again.

In order to continue his presence among us,
Jesus promised to send us his Spirit of peace and
unity.
We ask that this Spirit be here with us now
as we join with your Son
in offering this sign of your faithfulness.

Father, may we, in this same spirit of faithfulness,
minister to the needs of your Church
and of men and women everywhere.
May our words and actions
always proclaim the Lordship of your Son, Jesus
Christ.

Through him,
with him,
in him,
in the unity of the Holy Spirit,
all glory and honor is yours,
almighty Father,
for ever and ever.
Amen.

James Tures, S.J.

9. SALVATION

We thank you, Father,
for the heavens and the earth you created,
for the lights in the firmament,
    the waters of the seas,
    the dry earth.
For the fish swarming in the oceans,
    the birds gliding through the skies,
    the animals creeping upon the ground.
For ourselves,
    created in your image,
    man and woman,
    blessed,
    and given dominion over your creation.

We thank you, Father, for calling us together,
for calling us in Abraham,
    away from our country,
    away from our kindred,
    away from our father's house,
to a new land which you would show us.
For calling us in Moses,
    from the oppressors of Egypt,
    from the wilderness in the desert,
    from the worship of golden calves,
into a land flowing with milk and honey.
For calling us in prophecy,
    out of our adultery with false gods,
    out of slavery to Babylon,
    out of the valley of graveyards,
and into the fields and vineyards
which you had planted upon our land.

We thank you, Father,
that you can save us from blood-guilt,
that you can save us from the blood of Gettysburg,
    the blood of Hiroshima,
    the blood of My Lai;
that you can save us from the guilt of our rotting
    slums,
    the guilt of our squalid weapons,
    the guilt of our suffocating apathy;
that you can save us from the secret guilts
that fester inside the hearts of each of us.
But most of all, Father,
we thank you for your Son.
Through him we were created,
by him we have been called,
in him we shall be saved.

He made his home among us proclaiming:
The kingdom of God is here.
When he came the blind suddenly saw
and the lame walked.
Lepers were cleansed
and the deaf heard.
The dead were raised up
and the poor had the good news preached to them.

On the night before he died
he shared a meal with his friends.
He took some bread,
he gave you thanks,
he broke it,
he gave it to them saying:
Here is my body given for you.

And then he took a cup of wine,
gave you thanks, and said:
Here is the new covenant in my blood.
Do this in remembrance of me.

It is in thanksgiving, Father,
that in gathering around this table
we do remember how after his death you raised him
        up for us,
and in thanksgiving we once more eat that meal,
the meal that creates us again in your love,
        that calls us together into brotherhood,
        that saves us through this bread and wine.

In thanks, therefore, we proclaim the mystery of
        faith:
        Dying you destroyed our death,
        rising you restored our life.
        Lord Jesus, come in glory.

We pray, Father,
that your Holy Spirit may fill us
so that we may share the gift of your love,
        which creates,
        which calls,
        which saves,
the love that we have seen in the face of Jesus Christ.

For we now know
that neither death nor life,
    neither things present nor things to come,
    nor anything else in all creation,
can separate us from the love of God our Father,
who together with his Spirit,
shines in Christ Jesus our Lord.

    Through him,
    with him,
    in him,
    in the unity of the Holy Spirit,
    all glory and honor is yours,
    almighty Father,
    for ever and ever.
    Amen.

Manuel Velasquez, S.J.

10. HEALING

Father, we, your children,
give you thanks and praise.

We praise you for being our God,
for creating us in your image
and making us your people.

We bless you because your love for us is not hidden
but revealed in all your works:
in cool water that quenches our thirst,
in gentle rain that nourishes our parched earth,
in unexpected clouds that shade us
from the heat of noonday sun,
in refreshing breezes and evening winds,
in sunrises and the hope they bring,
in the challenge of new and unforeseen encounters and
events,
and in sunsets that bring an end to long hard days.

We thank you, Father, that your response
to our ingratitude, is your definitive word
of forgiveness and love: Jesus Christ.
He came and shared our life
in all its complexity,
with all its ambiguity.

We thank you, Father, because
when we and our world were an open wound,
you sent your word of healing to us: Jesus Christ.
He opened the eyes of the blind.
He unsealed the ears of the deaf.
He taught the lame to walk again
and the mute to sing for joy.

We thank you, Father, that Jesus took upon himself
our sickness and confusion.
He made us whole and gave our lives direction.

He healed us of our emptiness by giving us a meal.
On the night before he died
he gathered his friends together.
At supper, he took some bread
and gave you thanks.
He broke the bread
and passed it among them saying:
Take this, all of you, and eat.
This is my body given up for you.

Then he took the cup of wine
and praised your name.
He gave the cup to them, saying:
Take this, all of you, and drink.
This is the cup of my blood,
poured out for you and for all men,
so sins may be forgiven.
It is an everlasting covenant.
Do this in memory of me.

We thank you, Father, for Christ's life among us,
the way he cured us of our selfishness
by teaching us to love.
We thank you for his death, the living out of love.
We gratefully recall the hope we have
in Jesus' resurrection and ascension,
the hope of new and fuller life.

Together, then, as believers of this paschal event,
we proclaim the mystery of our faith:
>Lord, by your cross and resurrection,
>you have set us free.
>You are the Savior of the world.

Send us your Spirit, Father,
with all his power to heal.
Where we are fragmented, make us whole;
where we are desperate, help us walk in hope;
where we are many, make us always one.

Teach us to share with all people
the healing and forgiveness you have shared with us.
Help us work to cure the illness of our world—
the hatred, envy, greed and pride
that keep us apart—
so that one day all men can live in peace
and be, as you created us,
children of your love,
and instruments of healing for one another.

All this we ask through Christ, your Son,
who is our health and salvation.

    Through him,
    with him,
    in him,
    in the unity of the Holy Spirit,
    all glory and honor is yours,
    almighty Father,
    for ever and ever.
    Amen.

Michael Moynahan, S.J.

11. CONSOLATION

We praise you and thank you, Father in heaven.
You are the source of all contentment.

When we are in anguish, you wipe away our tears.
When we are in pain, you heal our afflictions.
When we grieve, you stand by us.
When we suffer injustice, you strengthen us.
When we are alone, you come to us.

You love us faithfully.
You have compassion on our needs.

We are your children, Father,
the little ones you have chosen.
Be pleased, then, with the prayer
which we now offer to you as we say:

      Holy, holy, holy Lord . . .

We praise you and thank you for Jesus, our Lord.
For he has borne our griefs and shared our sorrows.
He has cleansed and healed us by the touch of his
      hand.
He is the spotless Lamb who takes away the sins of
      the world.
He breathes into our hearts the Holy Spirit, the
      Comforter.
His gift is peace.

We recall that on the night
he was betrayed by one whom he loved,
he took bread into his hands.
He blessed you, Father, for your goodness.
And he gave the bread to his friends with the words:
Take this and eat it.
This is my body which will be given up for you.

Then he took a cup of wine.
Again he blessed you for your love.
And he gave the cup to his disciples with the words:
Take this and drink from it, all of you.
This is the cup of my blood,
the blood of the new and everlasting covenant.
It will be shed for you and for everyone
for the forgiveness of sins.
Do this in memory of me.

Father, we remember
how Jesus suffered grievously for our sins.
But by his wounds we are healed.
For we share in the joy of his resurrection.
And we are waiting to welcome him when he returns
    in glory.

Console us, then, by the power of his Spirit.
Teach us to bear with one another in love.
Give us joy in serving you
and in comforting all whom you send us.
Make us worthy of the gift of your Son.

Through him,
with him,
in him,
in the unity of the Holy Spirit,
all glory and honor is yours,
almighty Father,
for ever and ever.
Amen.

Donald Gelpi, S.J.

12. CREATION

Blessed are you, Father, God of all creation.

In the beginning your Spirit hovered over the earth
and called into being every creature that exists.

Earth itself responded to your love
and to every creature that came to be,
you said: Yes, you are good.

The waters brought forth life.
Into clay you breathed a living soul.
From that day man has sung your praise.

There is nothing that is not drawn to you
for the glory of your presence is written on all that is.
You are reflected in high mountains and lowly
      valleys.
You are there in the deep oceans and the farthest
      stars
and in the stirrings of our hearts.

So we thank you, Father, and give you praise
for every cup of water given in your name,
for the joy of every child who comes into the world,
and for every person who has touched us with your
      presence.

We blend our voices with the prayer of all creation
as we sing your praise with words that shall never
   cease:

   Holy, holy, holy Lord . . .

Father, we thank you especially for Jesus.
In the fullness of time,
you sent him in your name to draw us ever closer to
   you.

He emptied himself and became as all men are,
and being as all men are, he was humbler yet,
even to accepting death, death on a cross.

You raised him high,
setting him above all creation,
so that every tongue should acclaim:
Jesus Christ is Lord.
It was for us you did this,
so that we may give you glory
filled with the fullness of your love.

In the spirit and example of Jesus,
we are gathered here to celebrate this meal,
to become a living sign of your presence in our
   world.
We recall that he took bread and thanked you for
   your constant love.
He broke the bread, and gave it to his friends,
   saying:
Take this and share it among you.
This is my body given for you.

He also took the cup of wine.
Again he gave you praise
and shared it with those who were with him, saying:
Take this and drink from it, all of you.
This is the cup of the new covenant in my blood,
shed for people everywhere.
Whenever you do this, do it in memory of me.

And so, Father, we recall his life and death,
his rising from the dead,
and his ascension to your right hand.
You have made him Lord,
and we now join our life with his,
a perfect prayer,
responding to your boundless love.

With great joy, let us proclaim the mystery of our
    faith:
    When we eat this bread and drink this cup,
    we proclaim your death, Lord Jesus,
    until you come in glory.

Father, send your Spirit upon us,
so that we who eat this bread and share this cup
may become one people
nourished by your love.

We pray that by the action of this same Spirit,
we may know that all people are our brothers and
     sisters,
so that wherever we are
peace and justice will be the signs of your presence
     among us.
We make our prayer in the name of Christ Jesus, our
     Lord.

Through him,
with him,
in him,
in the unity of the Holy Spirit,
all glory and honor is yours,
almighty Father,
for ever and ever.
Amen.

Ron Wolf, S.J.

13. COVENANT

The vivid and concrete imagery of this prayer makes it ideal for showing slides simultaneously during its proclamation.

It is right and just,
our duty and privilege
always and everywhere
to give you thanks and praise, almighty Father.

You alone have shown yourself to be the God of life
by entering into covenant with all your living
        creatures.
You lead the whole of creation to salvation
in these signs of your covenant ever recurring:
from nothing to creation,
across flood to mountain-top,
through sea to dry land,
up from slavery to freedom,
off desert to green pastures
after fast to feast,
past war to peace.

You care for the world, guiding it
from sickness to health,
beyond night to day
up from seed to blooming tree,
from rain to shine,
over winter to spring-time,
by cross to crown,
out of grave to glory.

In this litany of your mighty deeds
we proclaim your loyalty,
we remember your steadfast love
and faithfulness to your covenant promises,
and we join our voices with the whole of creation
to sing your praise and glory:

Holy, holy, holy Lord . . .

In particular, today, eternal Father,
we typify our salvation history
by recalling a single event within our Jewish heritage.
Because Noah found favor in your eyes,
you saved a few of our ancestors and other living
        creatures
from the destruction of the forty day flood.

We are those descendants of Noah with whom you
        promised
to establish a lasting covenant,
and we see in the vault of heaven
the rainbow you have set as a sign
of that first saving pledge.
In later days, fulfilling that prophecy of salvation,
you sent Jesus, your beloved Son,
in whom, also, you were well pleased,
that in his life, death and rising,
he would be that new and everlasting covenant.

As a sign of this new covenant of life and love,
Jesus, on the night before he suffered and died,
gathered his friends for the final passover meal.
Over the bread and wine,
he remembered your many saving acts, and said:
Take and eat and drink.
This is my body broken for you,
this is my blood poured out for your sins.
Do this in memory of me
as the sign of the new and everlasting covenant.

Father, with these signs, we remember
that Jesus suffered, died, rose from the dead
and returned to your glory.
In the spirit of your Son's prayer,
we surrender our lives to you
by eating and drinking your covenantal meal of
        bread and wine.

Let us proclaim the mystery of our faith:
        When we eat this bread and drink this cup,
        we proclaim your death, Lord Jesus,
        until you come in glory.

As you commanded Noah to gather his small family
and other living creatures into the ark
to ride safe and dry over the flood waters,
so Jesus has gathered all of us, his family,
into the Church through the waters of baptism,
into his death and resurrection,
where we, too, have died to sin
and been raised to new life in his Spirit,
nourished by the one bread.

Send us again the Spirit of our baptism
who helps us through prayer and repentance
to overcome the sin in our lives.
May we always preach the good news of your
    kingdom
and the resurrection of life in Jesus Christ.

    Through him,
    with him,
    in him,
    in the unity of the Holy Spirit,
    all glory and honor is yours,
    almighty Father,
    for ever and ever.
    Amen.

Kevin Maxwell, S.J.

14. GOD'S PRESENCE

This thanksgiving prayer employs the liturgical principle of
proclamation and response. The celebrant proclaims a section
of the prayer and the congregation responds in word or song
with their assent. In keeping with the form of the eucharistic
prayer, the response of the congregation is always one of praise
addressed to the Father. Other suitable acclamations can also
be used.

Cel.
By your creative word, Father,
you established us
and all things in your saving presence.
You walked in the garden
in the cool of the evening,
and promised mankind freedom
from the bonds of evil.
You sent Moses to free your people
and he drew courage from your name and your
        promise:
"I am the one who will be with you."

Cong.
We give you thanks, Father, and we praise you
because from the beginning of time
you have been with us, and you are with us now.

Cel.
When you sent Isaiah to comfort your people,
you told him: "I have called you by name
and you are mine . . . fear not, for I am with you."
To Jeremiah's protest you answered:
"Be not afraid . . . for I am with you to deliver
        you,"

and you sent him to proclaim the new covenant
to be written on the hearts of men.
Through a messenger, your word to Mary was:
"Hail, favored one, the Lord is with you,"
and by the overshadowing of your Spirit
the Word of your presence,
Emmanuel,
took flesh and made his dwelling in our midst.

Cong.
Refrain.

Cel.
We truly give you thanks, Father,
because your Word, Jesus,
by his life and by the wonders he worked among us,
spoke your love
and proclaimed your presence in our world.
He gave sight to the blind,
and his word to us was: "I am the light of the
        world."
He told the lame to get up and walk,
and proclaimed: "I am the way, and the truth, and
        the life."
He opened our deaf ears,
revealed you as Father
and helped us realize we are your children.
He told his followers: "I am the resurrection and the
        life,"
and when he raised Lazarus from the dead
he spoke to us of the freedom we are given
to live always in your loving presence.

Cong.
Refrain.

Cel.
And finally, he called us friends
and gave the great proof of his love
by giving up his life for us.
We remember that at the final meal
he shared with his disciples,
on the night he was betrayed,
Jesus took bread,
and when he had given you thanks,
he broke it, and said,
"This is my body, broken for you.
Do this in remembrance of me."

In the same way after supper,
he took the cup, praised your name, and said:
"This cup is the new covenant in my blood,
shed for you and for all.
Do this, as often as you drink it,
in remembrance of me."

And so we come together, Father,
to remember
the life of your Word, Jesus, among us.
We celebrate his gift of life to us
through his dying and rising,
his return to you
and his sending of the Holy Spirit among us.

This is the mystery of your great faithfulness:
your abiding, saving, and comforting presence
in our lives, and for this we give you thanks.

Cong.
Refrain.

Cel.
Open us up, Father,
to receive the Spirit of your Son.
Joined to the worship Jesus offers you,
may we be brought together in community.
Let our sharing of the body and blood of Jesus
keep us united always.
May the life of our community
be a sign to all
that you are a loving God
and worthy of all praise.

Together we proclaim the saving name of Jesus
and make our prayer in his spirit of love.
> Through him,
> with him,
> in him,
> in the unity of the Holy Spirit,
> all glory and honor is yours,
> almighty Father,
> for ever and ever.
> Amen.

Paul Rōy, S.J.

15.   LIGHT

This prayer is dialogic in form. It permits a more active eucharistic participation for the congregation.

Cel.
Father, we praise you and bless you
because you do not hide from us,
but reveal yourself clearly in creation.

Cong.
All your works proclaim
love and concern for us.
We thank you for these gifts.

Cel.
For being a Father of Light
and sharing your brilliance with us,
we give you thanks.

Cong.
You created us in your image,
you made us to walk in light.
But we sinned.
Confused and often lost,
we preferred to walk in darkness.

Cel.
We thank you, Father,
that we cannot hide from you,
that you seek us out and find us
even in our darkness.

Cong.
So we join all of creation,
that basks in your love,
in proclaiming your glory as we say:

Holy, holy, holy Lord . . .

Cel.
We thank you, Father, for appointing your Son
as a covenant to the people,
a Light for all nations,
He has come to open the eyes of the blind,
to free captives from prison
and to bring into the Light
all who dwell in darkness.

Cong.
Your Light, Jesus Christ,
has penetrated our darkness
and shown us the way
from selfishness to love
from isolation to community, from death to life.
We thank you, Father, that Jesus is our Light
and has called us to be lights of the world.
We thank you for his life and example.

Cel.
But most of all, we thank you, Father,
for the wonderful way Jesus strengthens us
to be lights for the world.

Cong.

On the night before he died,
Jesus gathered his friends together.
He reminded them where they came from
and what they were to be.
He strengthened them for their mission
through a meal.

Cel.

While they were at supper he took some bread,
blessed you, Father, and gave it to them saying:
Take this and eat, all of you.
This is my body given up for you.

Then he took the cup filled with wine.
Again he thanked you, Father,
and gave it to them saying:
Take this and drink, all of you.
This is the cup of my blood
poured out for you and all men
so sins may be forgiven.
Do this in memory of me.

Cong.

Gratefully, we remember Jesus' life among us,
a life of light and love.
We remember in Jesus' suffering and death
the cost of being a light for one another.
And finally, we constantly call to mind
the hope of a new and fuller life
where darkness is dispelled forever.

Cel.
And so together we proclaim our paschal faith:
> Christ has died,
> Christ is risen,
> Christ will come again.

Send us, Father, the Spirit Jesus promised us:
the Spirit that gives direction to our weary feet
and light to our pilgrim-path.
Help us discover the places where you dwell.
Open our eyes to your presence in us,
our brothers, our sisters, and our world.

Cong.
Finally, we pray that through this meal
we may be strengthened in our resolve
to become more what you want us to be:
your community of love
and lights to the world.

Cel.
All of this we ask through Christ, our Light.
> Through him,
> with him,
> in him,
> in the unity of the Holy Spirit,
> all glory and honor is yours,
> almighty Father,
> for ever and ever.
> Amen.

Michael Moynahan, S.J.

16. FIRE

We praise you and thank you, Father in heaven.
Your holy love is a consuming fire.
Your word is a living flame.
By your prophets you kindle our hope.

In the fire of judgment you visit your people.
You purify our hearts.
Your anger blazes at the injustice of men.
You are faithful to your little ones.

You test us in the crucible of sorrow.
You confirm us in fidelity.
You kindle in us the fire of your zeal.
You send us to witness to your love.

When it is dark, you are our light.
When it is cold and desolate, you are our warmth.
We thank you for your great mercy.
And we join our voices to those
who know you and praise you as we say:

       Holy, holy, holy Lord . . .

We thank you, Father, for Jesus, our Lord.

He came to cast fire upon the earth.
And his heart blazed until it was kindled.
He has baptized us with the flames of his Spirit.
He has sealed your eternal covenant of love.

We recall that on the night he was betrayed,
he took bread into his hands and gave you thanks.
He broke the bread and said:
Take this and eat it, all of you.
For this is my body which will be given up for you.

Then he took a cup of wine.
He blessed you for your love.
And he gave the cup to his friends with the words:
Take this and drink of it, all of you.
For this is the cup of my blood,
the blood of the new and everlasting covenant.
It will be shed for you and for all
so that sins may be forgiven.
Do this in memory of me.

Father, we remember that Jesus suffered and died
so that we might not perish
in the sea of unquenchable fire.
We tested him.
But he was faithful to your call.
You raised him to life.
And he shall come again to judge the living and the
    dead.

Until that day,
purify our hearts by the power of his Spirit.
Burn away our sins.
And so strengthen us that we may welcome him
in joy and love when he appears.

Through him,
with him,
in him,
in the unity of the Holy Spirit,
all glory and honor is yours,
almighty Father,
for ever and ever.
Amen.

Donald Gelpi, S.J.

17. WATER

We praise you and thank you, Father in heaven.
You have led us to the water of life.
Before the earth was made,
you breathed upon the deep.
You made dry land appear.

You bless the earth with life-giving rain.
You make the wasteland bloom.
You are the Lord of the storm and of the flood.
You speak and they are still.

You cleanse us with the waters of forgiveness.
You wash away our sins.
From the rock you make living water spring.
You quench the thirst of your people.

Father, we thank you,
we acknowledge your great love.
And with all of your works
we proclaim your glory as we say:

     Holy, holy, holy Lord . . .

We praise you, Father, for your Son, Jesus Christ.
He is the Lord of the waves, he is master of
    confusion.
He speaks and they subside.
By the water of regeneration he cleanses our
    iniquities.

He gives us new life.
He is the rock from whom living waters flow.
He pours forth your Spirit upon all flesh.

Father, in the power of his Spirit
we have gathered in your name.
And we recall that on the night he was betrayed,
Jesus took bread. He thanked you.
Then as a sign of his love he broke the bread
and gave it to his disciples with the words:
Take this and eat it.
This is my body which will be given up for you.

Then he took a cup of wine.
Again he thanked you.
And he gave it to his disciples with the words:
Take this and drink from it, all of you.
This is the cup of my blood,
the blood of the new and everlasting covenant.
It will be shed for you
for the forgiveness of sins.
Do this in memory of me.

Father, we remember that Jesus loved us.
He died for us.
But you raised him from death and revealed him as
    Lord.
Teach us to die with him
that we too may share in the fullness of his life.
Baptize us in the living water of his Spirit
and unite us and all men and women in his peace.

Through him,
with him,
in him
in the unity of the Holy Spirit,
all glory and honor is yours,
almighty Father,
for ever and ever.
Amen.

Donald Gelpi, S.J.

18.   FREEDOM

Almighty Father,
we praise and bless you
because you are a God of freedom.

You created us above all other creatures
and gave us this earthly paradise to enjoy.
Instead, we close the forbidden fruit of sin.
But you did not abandon us,
and again offered freedom through your love.

We bless you, Father, that you remained mindful
of your promise to Abraham.
You bade Moses to lead Israel
out of the slavery of Egypt.
He led your nation
through the Red Sea and Sinai Desert
to a new land of freedom,
a land flowing with milk and honey.

We praise you, Father, for your prophets
who, countless times, urged your people
to break the chain of idolatry to foreign gods.
You constantly call us from submission
to images of stone which cannot hear or understand
to growth in your spirit of love.

And so, with hearts full of confidence
we join your holy people,
who stand in the freedom of your presence,
and sing to you the ancient hymn of holiness
        and glory:

        Holy, holy, holy Lord . . .

Father, you are the source of all holiness.
You call us to live in the light
and freedom of your Spirit.

In our need of liberation,
you sent your Son to be
the way, the truth, and the life.
He freed us from our divisions
by inviting us to love our neighbor.
He liberated us from our selfishness
by encouraging us to give freely
of what we have freely received:
our talents, our riches, our time.

Father, we remember your Son's
great sign of love for us.
On the night before he suffered
in order to free us from our sins,
he celebrated a meal of life and hope.
He took bread and blessed you, his almighty Father;
he broke the bread, and gave it to his friends saying:
Take this, all of you, and eat it;
this is my body which is given up for you.

At the end of the meal, he took the cup of blessing.
Once again, he gave you thanks and praise.
He gave the cup to his friends and said:
Take this, all of you, and drink.
This is the cup of liberation,
the new covenant in my blood
which is shed for you and for all people
so that sins may be forgiven.
Do this in memory of me.

Father, we recall to mind the life, death,
resurrection and return to your glory
of our Savior and Lord, Jesus Christ.
In the spirit of his perfect worship to you,
join us in his praise
as we surrender our lives to you
through this bread of life and cup of covenant.

Let us now proclaim our liberation in Christ:
   Lord, by your cross and resurrection
   you have set us free.
   You are the Savior of the world.

Father, send your Spirit upon us
so that we who are nourished at your table
may witness in love to the needs of our neighbors.
Help us to grow in the freedom of the children of
   God
so that we may not be chained to
status, honor, or money.
May we imitate the life of your Son
by freeing ourselves and others
from the bondage of oppression and injustice.

As you welcome all peoples into your kingdom
so may we see the dignity of your reflection
in everyone we meet.
May your Holy Spirit rule our governments
and especially our homes and hearts.

We make our prayer in the name of Jesus Christ
who is the liberator of the world.
>   Through him,
>   with him,
>   in him,
>   in the unity of the Holy Spirit,
>   all glory and honor is yours,
>   almighty Father,
>   for ever and ever.
>   Amen.

John Mossi, S.J.

19. MERCY

We thank you, almighty Father,
and we give you praise
because you are Lord
of our deserts and our ashes.
You loved us and sent your Son
to turn our deserts to gardens,
our ashes to his new fire.
He has given us life
and taught us to hope,
because he has shown that you are our Father,
and so we give you thanks
and join your whole creation
in a hymn of praise, singing:

    Holy, holy, holy Lord . . .

We thank you, almighty God,
because your saving actions
have from the very beginning
given us the promise of life.
As Father, you have not neglected our plight
nor left us to die by the wages of our sin.
You have not given us ashes to eat like bread
nor tears to mingle with our wine.

Despite our sins, you have called us
from slavery to a promised land,
from exile to a New Jerusalem,
from law to freedom.

Finally, though we set our hearts against you
by sin and idolatry and despair,
you did not turn away your face
but promised us a Messiah.

And so you sent your only Son
to share all our sorrows
of desert and ashes and death.
He centered our hopes
by his works and words among us.

And then on the night before he died
he called his friends together a final time.
He took bread and wine,
and praised you, his almighty Father.
He gave the broken bread and cup to all and said:
This is my body, broken for you,
and my blood, shed for you and all people
so that sins may be forgiven.
Whenever you do this,
you will do it in memory of me.

And now, Father, we remember and celebrate
how Jesus conquered death
by his own passion and dying
and how he gave us life
by his resurrection and gift of the Spirit.

Let us proclaim the mystery of our faith:
Dying you destroyed our death,
rising you restored our life.
Lord Jesus, come in glory.

Send your Holy Spirit, Lord,
to breathe upon the gifts and meal
which we share in your sight.
May we partake of this living bread
and this living cup as men and women
unified with the one Church of Christ.
We pray that we may be signs
of your new covenant
anointed with the Spirit's new fire of love
in Christ Jesus our Lord.
Through him,
with him,
in him,
in the unity of the Holy Spirit,
all glory and honor is yours,
almighty Father,
for ever and ever.
Amen.

Stephen Kuder, S.J.

20. CALL

Blessed are you, Father, God of all creation.
Through your goodness, you have made this world
and called us to be your children.

We thank you for the sun, the moon,
this earth, and its birds, fish, trees,
and everything that is beautiful around us.

We thank you especially for our freedom,
for the dreams of the young and for old men's
       visions,
for our minds, our hearts, our bodies.

We praise you, for you call us to build the earth
into a community of love.
This will be our prayer to you.

You have placed confidence in us,
for you have made us
and you know that we are good.

In joy, and in thanksgiving for your call to us,
we join with all creation as we sing your praise
in words that shall never cease:

    Holy, holy, holy Lord . . .

Father, we do not always understand
what you have planned for us.
It is difficult to grasp
the mysterious depths of your love.

So you sent your Son, Jesus,
to show us who we are.
He challenged us to call you Father
and taught us not to be afraid.
He showed us how to forgive
and taught us that love is stronger than all sin.

And so, Father, to help us remember the call
you have given us,
we gather here at Jesus' command,
to celebrate this simple meal.

We recall that on the night before he died,
Jesus took bread, and giving thanks to you, Father,
he blessed it, broke it and shared it with his friends,
    saying:
Take this and eat it, all of you.
This is my body, broken for you.

In the same way he took a cup of wine,
again giving thanks to you, Father.
He blessed it and shared it among his friends, saying:
Take this and drink from it, all of you,
for this is the cup of the new covenant in my blood
which is shed for you.
Do this in memory of me.

And so, Father, celebrating his death,
his rising from the dead
and ascension to your right hand,
we join in his perfect offering to you,
a life of love, lived in your presence.

Let us proclaim our salvation:
> When we eat this bread and drink this cup,
> we proclaim your death, Lord Jesus,
> until you come in glory.

Father, open our hearts to your Spirit dwelling
> within us.
May this same Spirit help us listen without fear
to your call to us.
May he lead us to a life of love and service,
full of confidence in you.

We pray
that wherever we are, justice will shine forth,
and that all men and women can approach each
> other as equals,
as brothers and sisters living in the light of your
> presence.

We make our prayer through Christ our Lord
through whom we receive everything that is good.

Through him,
with him,
in him,
in the unity of the Holy Spirit,
all glory and honor is yours,
almighty Father,
for ever and ever.
Amen.

Ron Wolf, S.J.

21.   A PRAYER FOR CHILDREN

This brief eucharistic prayer is especially composed for children age four to seven. It is simple in approach and theology, yet at the same time introduces the children to the traditional congregational responses.

God our Father,
we thank you
for you are a God of love and kindness.
You are interested in us,
your children.

With your children everywhere
we praise you for your goodness saying:

Holy, holy, holy Lord . . .

Father,
thank you for sharing your love
by sending people into our lives
to take care of us:
our parents, our brothers and sisters,
our neighbors, our friends.
Thank you for sending your Son, Jesus,
to be our close friend and brother.

He called us your little ones
and invited us to come to you
to be near you always.
So we can live in him more fully
he shared his life with us
in the food of bread and wine.

At a special meal
with his friends seated at table,
Jesus took bread,
and gave you thanks, Father, for your great goodness.
He broke the bread and said:
I want you to eat this bread,
for this bread is my body which will be given up for
      you.

Then Jesus took a cup of wine and said:
This cup of wine is the sign of the new friendship
in my blood which is poured out for you
and for all people.
Do this in memory of me.

We remember Jesus' concern for us
by his coming into our world
as our friend and brother.
We remember that he died, and rose from the dead
so that he would be closer to us
through his Spirit.

Let us proclaim the gift of God's love:
    Christ has died,
    Christ is risen,
    Christ will come again.

Father, send the Spirit of Jesus to be our helper
so that our actions will be like the actions of Jesus.

May we treat others
as we would like them to treat us.
May we be a real friend,
a brother or sister,
to anyone who feels lost, alone, or in need.

We make our prayer with our brother, Jesus.
    Through him,
    with him,
    in him,
    in the unity of the Holy Spirit,
    all glory and honor is yours,
    almighty Father,
    for ever and ever.
    Amen.

Tony Fromhart, S.J.
John Mossi, S.J.

22. ADVENT

Father, all powerful and ever-living God,
you are worthy of glory and praise.
Out of your generosity, creation came into being,
the vast expanse of space, suns, planets,
and this earth, our home.
Father, from the earth
you brought forth mankind
and clothed him with humor and imagination.

You have made us rulers of all creation.
But we betrayed your trust,
and refused to recognize your presence in each other.

With fatherly concern,
you called us to return to you.
The prophets, bursting with your message,
urged us to seek forgiveness of our sins.
Finally, in the fullness of time
your all-powerful Word, Jesus Christ, became man.

By his death and rising
all of us share in your life, Father,
and we wait with joy and eager expectation
for your Son's coming in glory.
Until that day,
we join hands with all creation around your table,
and praise you in the words of your prophet Isaiah:

Holy, holy, holy Lord . . .

We give you thanks, Father,
for the life of your Son, Jesus Christ.
He leveled the mountains of ignorance and injustice.
He stretched the visions of our beliefs
far beyond their normal horizons.
He readily forgave our sins.

Your Son extended the hope of salvation
by inviting all people to sit at table with you.
On the night before he died,
he gathered together his friends for a final meal.

While at supper,
he took the bread and gave you thanks.
He broke the bread
and shared it saying:
Take and eat.
This is my body which will be broken for you.

At the end of the meal,
Jesus took wine,
praised your fidelity, Father,
and passed the cup to his disciples saying:
Take and drink,
this is the cup of the new covenant in my blood.
It will be shed for you and for all men
so that sins may be forgiven.
Do this in memory of me.

Father, we make present the life of your Son.
He was broken and crushed for us.
He passed through pain into your hands at death.
But through the power of your Spirit,
you raised him to life again.
He is the first-born of creation.
He is the dawn from on high
who will forever break into our world
and remove fear from all
who dwell in darkness and the shadow of death.
He guides us to everlasting peace
through the power of your Holy Spirit.

With confidence and joy,
let us proclaim God's saving action through Christ:
    Lord, by your cross and resurrection
    you have set us free.
    You are the Savior of the world.

May this food
which we are about to share with one another
express our thanks to you.
Enliven in us the presence of your Spirit.
Only with his help can we lift up our eyes
and see that your Son has loosed the bonds
of selfishness and sin,
uniting us as brothers and sisters in your Church.

Shower from the heavens your love, Father
so that your kingdom may take root and grow in our
    hearts.
Shatter the darkness in our lives with the light of
    your wisdom.

May our actions reflect your gentle love
as we await your full revelation in Jesus Christ.
    Through him,
    with him,
    in him,
    in the unity of the Holy Spirit,
    all glory and honor is yours,
    almighty Father,
    for ever and ever.
    Amen.

James Ditillo, S.J.

23. EMMANUEL

We praise you and thank you, Father in heaven.
You dwell among us by your faithful love.
Long ago you called your people from bondage.
Your tent was among them.
You led them to freedom.

You chose Jerusalem to be your home.
In the Holy Place you revealed your glory.
Through the lips of Isaiah you promised a savior.
You named him Emmanuel, God-with-us.

In the fullness of time you sent your Son.
Born of a virgin, he dwelt among men.
You anointed him with the Spirit of service.
By the Spirit, the Consoler, he dwells still among us.

Drawn by his Spirit, we gather before you.
We praise you, Father, and find joy in your presence
as we pray:

Holy, holy, holy Lord . . .

We thank you, Father, for Jesus, our Savior.
He is the image and the proof of your love.
He took on our flesh and shared our bread
so that we might live as your adoptive children.
He abides in our midst as our food and our life.
He is with us now and to the end of time.

We remember that on the night he was betrayed,
he gave us a sign of his faithful presence.
In the midst of his disciples he took bread.
He praised you, Father, for your love and mercy.
Then he broke the bread
and gave it to them with the words:
Take this and eat.
This is my body which will be given up for you.

Then he took the cup.
Again he blessed your name.
And he gave the cup to his friends with the words:
Take this and drink from it, all of you.
This is the cup of my blood,
the blood of the new and everlasting covenant.
It will be poured out for you and people everywhere
for the forgiveness of sins.
Do this in memory of me.

Father we thank you for sending us Jesus.
He died for our sins, but by his death we find life.
For you raised him in glory and revealed him as
        Lord.
In his risen body dwells the fullness of Godhead.

Transform us, then, into the temple of his Spirit.
Dwell in our praise, in our service, in our love.
Make us the sign of your presence to men.
And lead us all to the vision
of your glory through Jesus, our Lord.

Through him,
with him,
in him,
in the unity of the Holy Spirit,
all glory and honor is yours,
almighty Father,
for ever and ever.
Amen.

Donald Gelpi, S.J.

24. INCARNATION

Father, we gather together
and give you thanks
for all the wonders of your love.

We marvel at how you continue to lavish your gifts
     upon us,
life, health, family and friends,
when you constantly meet with ingratitude.
You truly deserve the name "Faithful One"
for your love is everlasting.

We thank you for all the signs of your love in our
     lives
which are more numerous than the grains of sandy
     beaches.

But especially, we thank you
for speaking your Word, Jesus Christ, to us.
You could have shown no greater love than by
     sharing
what you treasured most, Jesus Christ, your only
     Son,
your Word of love, the hope to which we cling.

We thank you for speaking your word despite our
     deafness,
for putting your word in our stubborn hearts.

Your word is life in many ways,
a forgiving word, a reassuring smile,
friends who walk mysteriously into our lives
and awaken good in us we never knew existed.

Your word is hope,
creativity, imagination, and new beginnings,
when we somehow start out again
from the ashes of defeat or disappointment.

Your word is yes to who we are and all we do
as we struggle to discover your presence
in ourselves and our world.

Your Word is Jesus Christ:
yesterday! today! and forever!

We thank you for Jesus' life
and all he taught us of your love.
And of all he said and did, we particularly thank you
for the meal he shared and asked us to celebrate
over and over until he comes again.
When he was at supper with friends he took the
        bread,
blessed you, Father, and broke the bread, saying:
Take and eat.
This is my body broken for you.

Then he took the cup of wine,
blessed you again, Father,
and passed it among them saying:

Take and drink, all of you.
This is the cup of my blood
poured out for all for the forgiveness of sins.
Do this in memory of me.

And so, Father, we thank you for your Son.
He has pitched his tent among us and shared our lot.
By his life he has shown us the way from isolation
    into community.
By his death he has shown us the way from
    selfishness to love.
And by his resurrection he has spoken the word of
    hope
for a new and fuller life.

Let us proclaim God's saving action:
    Christ has died,
    Christ is risen,
    Christ will come again.

Send us your Spirit, Father,
the Spirit of truth,
to open our eyes and ears:
to see you where we are afraid to look,
to hear you in voices
that offend our sensitive ears.

We seek you in the spectacular and extraordinary,
and you come to us poor,
hungry, thirsty, naked,
diseased, in prison, alone,
and as the least of our brothers.
Teach us to see you, hear you, touch you, know you,
where you really are,
and not where we would like you to be.

All this we ask through Christ, the Lord of life.
    Through him,
    with him,
    in him,
    in the unity of the Holy Spirit,
    all glory and honor is yours,
    almighty Father,
    for ever and ever.
    Amen.

Michael Moynahan, S.J.

25. INVITATION

Blessed are you, heavenly Father,
for you keep extending your call to us
even when we fail to answer.
We thank you
for approaching us in different ways
tailored to our personalities.

We thank you for calling Jacob,
who first wrestled with your messenger
and yielded to the power of your love;
for Jeremiah, who tried to ignore your presence
but found your persistent calling impossible to refuse;
for Isaiah, who accepted your difficult invitation
to return Israel to your praise;
for Elijah who heard your sound in the movement
of cool winds and gentle breezes;
for John the Baptist, who was led by your Spirit
to fearlessly preach the coming of the Lord;
for your Son's calling of ordinary people
like Peter, James, John, and us.

We thank you, Father,
for you still invite people to share in your life.
And so, with hearts full of love,
we join with your saints in proclaiming your praise:

    Holy, holy, holy Lord . . .

Father, we bless you for the life of your Son.
He, too, gradually came to realize
the dimensions of your call.
In the temple,
he spoke your word to the elders of the land.
In the desert,
he was tempted to power, honor, and glory,
but chose obedience to your will.
In towns and villages,
he forgave sinners
and preached your kingdom of mercy and justice.
When lawyers and scribes tried to test him,
your Son responded with a new commandment of
    love.

Jesus, on the night before he died,
asked that the cup of Gethsemane be withdrawn.
But in response to your bidding he drank that cup
just as earlier in the evening
he gave us the cup of life everlasting.

Gathered with his friends at table,
Jesus took bread and blessed you, his almighty
    Father.
He broke the bread and shared it, saying:
Take and eat.
This is my body which will be given up for you.

Then he took the cup, blessed you again, and said:
Take and drink.
This is the cup of the new covenant in my blood
which is poured out for you and for all people.
Do this in memory of me.

Father, we joyfully remember
that the cup of the table
overcame the cup of the garden,
for your Son not only died but rose
that we might have life.
To help us respond to your call
and guide us in your ways
he has sent the Holy Spirit as your gift.

Let us proclaim our life in your Spirit:
When we eat this bread and drink this cup,
we proclaim your death, Lord Jesus,
until you come in glory.

Father, we ask that your Spirit
may continue to fill us with your grace.
May our ears, eyes, and hearts
be open to your summons, to your call.

Be mindful of your people, Father;
especially be present to those who are imprisoned,
tormented by illness, physical and mental,
and who find it difficult to hear and to respond.
Help us to find you,
in stillness and in turmoil,
in pleasure and in business.
May we always imitate the care and concern
of your Son who is the Savior of the world.

Through him,
with him,
in him,
in the unity of the Holy Spirit,
all glory and honor is yours,
almighty Father,
for ever and ever.
Amen.

George Sullivan, S.J.
John Mossi, S.J.

26. PILGRIMS

Father of pilgrims,
we gather together to praise and bless you.
Your name is faithful one and your love is
        everlasting.
We have come to experience your love in many ways
as life's pilgrims.

We thank you for the Spirit you breathe into us,
a wandering Spirit,
for eyes that guide us,
for feet that plod the paths,
for occasional signposts when we have lost our way.

We thank you for your love
which gives our journey meaning and direction.
You bless us with your divine restlessness.
You prod us from our complacency.
You urge us down roads
we do not feel strong enough to travel.
You support us with fellow-travellers
who bolster us when we despair,
who refresh and renew us
when we think our last step is just that.

For all those pilgrims who have gone before us
and pointed the way to you,
for Noah, Abraham and Sarah, Moses and Miriam,
for David, Ruth, Esther, Solomon and Isaiah,
we give you thanks, Father.

But most of all we thank you
for your greatest pilgrim, Jesus Christ.
He is the way, the truth and the life.
He lights our path. He opens our eyes.
He does not abandon us in our need.
His journey led him to Jerusalem.
There he strengthened us with a meal
to follow in his footsteps.

On the night before he died,
Jesus took bread and blessed you, Father.
He gave it to his friends with these words:
Here is food for the journey.
Take this, all of you, and eat.
This is my body given up for you.

Later he took a cup of wine.
Again he blessed you
and gave it to his friends with these words:
Here is drink for the journey.
Take this and share it.
This is the cup of my blood,
the new and everlasting covenant.
It is shed for you and all men
so sins may be forgiven.
Do this in memory of me.

And so, Father, we thank you
for the words and example of your pilgrim, Jesus.
By his life he teaches us
to believe in you and life's journey.
By his death he shows us
the meaning of hope when we lose everything.

And by his resurrection he proclaims your love
which makes all weary, wrinkled pilgrims new.

So let us proclaim the mystery of our faith:
    Dying you destroyed our death,
    rising you restored our life.
    Lord Jesus, come in glory.

Father, send us your Spirit
so that we, your pilgrims,
can have light for our eyes, strength for our limbs,
and companionship on an otherwise lonely journey.

Help us accept the gifts you have given us.
Teach us to use them as we struggle
with the journey-out and the journey-in,
the mystery of your presence in us and our world.
May we seek you, meet you and know you
as we travel along the way.
All this we ask through Jesus Christ
who is our way to you.

    Through him,
    with him,
    in him,
    in the unity of the Holy Spirit,
    all glory and honor is yours,
    almighty Father,
    for ever and ever.
    Amen.

Michael Moynahan, S.J.

PART II: BREAD BROKEN

The Breaking of the Bread

The eucharistic words of institution over the bread and wine are familiar to all of us. Perhaps too familiar. Their liturgical prominence overpowers an equally significant aspect of the eucharist: its actions. Jesus, at the Last Supper, ritualized in a special way the four principal actions of that meal. He took bread, blessed it, broke it and shared it. These four actions of taking, blessing, breaking, and sharing are the liturgical basis for the preparation of the gifts, the eucharistic prayer, the breaking of the bread, and communion. A liturgy which fails to adequately ritualize these actions is deficient in its symbolic communication.

Throughout the history of the Church, these actions of taking, blessing, breaking, and sharing have experienced greater or lesser emphasis. The early Church highlighted the action of breaking bread. This particular action expressed the mystery of the community's new relationship to each other in Christ. The breaking of the one bread for communion was the perfect sign of unity. It represented the community's participation in the life of the Risen Lord and also their union with one another. "This bread which we break, is it not a participation in the body of Christ?" (1 Cor. 10:16)

What was a clear and meaningful religious action for the early Church has become an ambiguous gesture for us. Now that the Mass is celebrated facing the assembly, most people are aware that bread is broken in a eucharistic celebration, but how many know that this action conveys a special meaning? Or that the breaking of the bread is one of the essential actions of a eucharistic celebration? The lack of a proper historical appreciation as well as an insufficient understanding of the present liturgical emphasis given to the breaking of the bread creates significant problems on two levels, meaning and action. Ours is the task of reviving an action that during the past nine hundred years has become greatly impoverished and almost entirely lost.

Five New Testament passages underscore the importance and meaning of the breaking of the bread for the apostolic Church:

Institution Narrative
And as they were eating, he took bread, and blessed, and broke it, and gave it to them, and said, "Take; this is my body." (Mark 14:22)

Disciples at Emmaus
When he was at table with them, he took the bread and blessed and broke it, and gave it to them. And their eyes were opened and they recognized him. (Luke 24:30) Then they told what had happened on the road and how he was known to them in the breaking of the bread. (Luke 24:35)

Activities of the Early Church
And they devoted themselves to the apostles' teachings and fellowship, to the breaking of bread and the prayers. (Acts 2:42)

St. Paul
The cup of blessing which we bless, is it not a participation in the blood of Christ? The bread which we break, is it not a participation in the body of Christ? Because there is one bread, we who are many are one body, for we all partake of the one bread. (I Cor. 10:16-17)

The New Testament writers record that Jesus broke bread at the Last Supper. The early Church, in obedience to his command, remembered him in the same way. They too broke bread at their eucharists. Since the breaking action belonged to the Lord, the early Church "recognized" Jesus in the breaking of the bread. Thus, every time they broke bread, it was an analogous way of remembering Jesus and making present his life and words. The breaking of the bread became one of the unambiguous signs of the presence of Christ among the community. Because the sign value of breaking bread was so obvious to the early Christians, the disciples at Emmaus were able to tell the others "how he was known to them in the breaking of the bread."

St. Paul, reflecting on the theological meaning of the breaking of the bread in I Cor. 10:16-17, shows that this was the sign of union for the assembly. The dramatic action of breaking the one bread was the clear gesture that all are intimately bound in the body of Christ, the Church.

As the Church grew, the Mass and the breaking of the bread became more ritualized. In the Masses of the sixth century, the faithful supplied leavened breads for the eucharist. These loaves were placed on large patens the size of trays and were brought to the altar at the presentation of the gifts. Then, to facilitate the breaking of these breads, deacons and subdeacons assisted the celebrant at the fraction. Acolytes in turn helped with the distribution of the bread at communion. It was at this time that the "Agnus Dei" was introduced as a hymnic accompaniment to the fraction rite.

However, by the tenth and eleventh century, the breaking of the bread became relegated to a position of secondary importance. The fraction rite slipped quietly into insignificance with the introduction of unleavened bread. Because these thin white hosts neither looked like nor tasted like bread, they were, and still are wherever they are used, an impoverished sign. These wafers, in turn, affected the meaning of the breaking of the bread. What used to occupy the attention of several ministers became reduced to the cracking of a single host. As a consequence, the action of breaking bread was lost. The introduction of unleavened bread also affected other aspects of the liturgy. The faithful no longer made the eucharistic bread for the Mass. The offertory procession, which was originally a time to bring forward the community's gifts for the poor and the bread for the eucharist developed into the collection of money for the support of the church. The large tray patens that held the community's bread were no longer necessary. These were replaced by the celebrant's paten which was the size of a very small bread plate.

As the ritual significance of the breaking of the bread and the other actions of the Mass became less and less transparent, attention centered on the host as the chief locus of the presence of Christ. Communion bread was no longer considered as a food to be eaten; instead it received increased reverence and adoration. By the eleventh century communion was given only on the tongue, contrary to the previously common practice of distribution in the hand. By the twelfth century the chalice ceased to be extended to the faithful and communion was administered to people kneeling.

In effect, the two eucharistic actions of breaking and sharing which were uppermost in the mind of the early Church almost completely disappeared. Not only was the meaning and action of the breaking of the bread obscured, but also the faithful participated less frequently in the full eucharistic meal. As a substitute for these principal actions of the eucharist, the consecrated host was held high for prolonged periods of time during the elevation. This became the focal point of the Mass.

Consequently, the early liturgy which was highly participatory and true to the actions of the Last Supper suffered major distortions. It became a ritual in which the language used (Latin) was unintelligible, and the meaning of its actions significantly clouded.

With the thrusts of Vatican II and Pope Paul VI's *General Instruction* and *The New Order of Mass*, a serious attempt to restore the prominence and meaning of the breaking of the bread has begun. The *Instruction*, in section 283 entitled "Requisites for Celebrating Mass," states:

> The nature of the sign demands that the material for the celebration appear as actual food. The eucharistic bread, even though unleavened and traditional in form, should therefore be made in such a way that the priest can break it and distribute the parts to at least some of the faithful. When the number of communicants is large or other pastoral needs require it, small hosts may be used. The gesture of the breaking of the bread, as the eucharist was called in apostolic times, will more clearly show the eucharist as a sign of unity and charity, since the one bread is being distributed among the members of one family.

Elsewhere, the *Instruction*, in section 56, referring to the breaking of the bread states:

> This gesture of Christ at the Last Supper gave the entire eucharistic action its name in apostolic times. In addition to its practical aspect, it signifies that in communion we who are many are made one body in the one bread which is Christ.

The *Instruction*, addressing those areas of the liturgy in need of updating, states that the bread "appear as actual food" so that it can be "broken" and "be distributed to at least some of the faithful." This is really an important step forward to rediscover the meaning of the eucharistic actions. The *Instruction* emphasizes that unleavened bread, not necessarily hosts, is to be used at Mass. Fortunately, there are a number of recipes available that produce a tasty and substantial bread that breaks easily. This homemade bread, like the homemade bread of the early Church, is the ideal bread to use. The norm that the *Instruction* suggests is that the eucharistic bread be distributed to "at least some of the faithful." This is the minimum requirement. The optimum is to distribute the eucharistic bread to all of the faithful. Small hosts may be used only "when the number of communicants is large or other pastoral needs require it." In effect, the *Instruction* restricts the use of small hosts. It suggests that the ideal is to imitate the practice of the first Christians by celebrating with real bread which more effectively communicates the rich meal symbolism of the Mass.

The *Instruction*, in section 293, which comments on sacred vessels, states:

> It is suitable to use one large paten for the consecration of the bread for the celebrant, ministers, and faithful.

Once again the restoration of the large paten, really the large plate or tray, is a return to another early Church practice. The large plate makes it easy for the one eucharistic bread or several eucharistic breads to be brought from the assembly and placed visibly together on the Lord's table. The visibility of the bread on the large plate is still another improvement over the diminished sign of hosts concealed in ciboria. It is important that the bread and wine be unobstructed by altar tabernacles, microphones, prayer cards, crucifixes, flowers, candles and other items that clutter the Lord's table. At all times the assembly should be able to see easily the bread and wine.

How can the action of breaking the bread be enhanced? Both adequate time and appropriate gesture should be given to the fraction in order to express fully its meaning. The celebrant should hold the bread over the plate for all to see while he slowly breaks it. In this way the bread is not only dramatically broken, but just as important, it is known to be broken by the members of the assembly. Preferably, this bread will be homemade by one of the congregation. While the bread is being broken, additional plates or baskets can be brought to the table thereby allowing other ministers to assist the celebrant in the fraction. The fraction rite continues until the necessary number of pieces are broken.

Similarly, if the cup is to be extended to the faithful, other chalices could be brought to the altar at the time of the fraction. The blessed wine which would be contained in a large decanter could then be poured into smaller chalices or crystal glasses for the concelebrants and assembly. In this manner the sign of unity and fellowship is achieved also with the wine. Everyone drinks from the wine blessed in the same vessel.

The prayers of this book are intended to enrich the meaning and articulation of the fraction rite. They can be proclaimed by the celebrant or another person while the bread is being broken. The prayers are of different lengths and styles so as to offer a variety to fit the needs of a particular celebration. The people can respond to the fraction prayer with a sung "Lamb of God" or a song containing a bread theme. The manner in which the breaking of the bread can be best ritualized will have to be adapted to the circumstances of each church. It is advisable that a period of instruction about the history and meaning of the breaking of the bread precede the re-emphasis of this rite.

Hopefully, through the use of these fraction prayers the breaking of the bread can be restored to its apostolic importance and be made a more meaningful sign of what we celebrate in the eucharist.

Prayers for the
Breaking of the Bread

A. BRIEF FRACTION RITES

1. BROKEN BREAD

Bread broken: one loaf but many pieces,
                  a meal for us.

Bread broken: divided that we might share it,
                  wholeness destroyed that we might be
                  joined together.

Bread broken: a sign of Christ's body,
                  broken for us that we might live.

2. NOURISHMENT

Loving Father,
you have fed us from our earliest days;
in your faithfulness,
nourish us today with the blessed bread of your
    Church,
bread broken so that all may share and grow
in the life-giving Spirit of your Son.

3. BLESSED AND BROKEN PEOPLE

May we become as this blessed bread, a blessed
    people,
blessed and broken in the love and care of one
    another.
We who eat of the same bread,
even though varied and different like its many grains
    of wheat,
are one in the body of Christ.

4. MANNA

Father, you once fed your people manna in the
    desert.
You now feed us with this bread of life.
May its many pieces broken from one loaf
be a reminder that we are a community of believers
dedicated to the service of one another.

5. ONE BREAD

Father, you give us golden fields of wheat
whose many grains we have gathered, milled,
and made into this one bread;
may the members of your Church
from north and south, east and west
be gathered into your kingdom.

6. FAMILY

When we break this bread and share this wine,
we declare that we are willing to see all people
as our brothers and sisters.
With God as our Father
we are members of his one family.

7. LIFE AND SPIRIT

The early Christians recognized
the life and spirit of Jesus
in the breaking of the bread.
In the tradition of their faith
and in imitation of their love,
we break this blessed bread,
recalling that at the Last Supper,
the Lord Jesus gave his body and blood to his friends
as a sign of oneness with them.

8.   I CORINTHIANS 11:26

Eternal Father,
you freely invite us to your kingdom of love and
        compassion.
May our sharing of this one cup and bread
be our pledge to live in your Spirit.
For when we eat this bread and drink this wine
we proclaim the death of the Lord Jesus
until he comes in glory.

9. BREAD OF LIFE

This bread which we break is the bread of life.
It is the sign of Christ's body prepared by the Father
and offered in sacrifice by the Son
in a spirit of obedience to the Father's will.
It is the sign of our unity with one another
in the Spirit of love and peace.

10. SIGN OF ONENESS

On a hillside in Galilee,
Jesus took bread, blessed it, broke it,
and gave it to his followers.
We, in like manner,
break the bread of the Lord
as a sign of our oneness,
as a sign of our desire
to share in the Father's heavenly banquet.

11. CREATION RENEWED

On this day of the Lord,
all creation is restored to your power
and renewed in your friendship.
As we break your holy food,
may we be imitators of your love
which has redeemed the world.

12. THE LORD'S BREAD

Jesus said, "I am the bread of life." (John 6:28)
The bread we now break is the Lord's blessed bread
divided into many pieces
so that we may share and live in his life.
For in the partaking of this bread,
we partake of his Spirit of love
and his promise of life-everlasting.

13. DIDACHE

As the elements of this broken bread,
once scattered over the mountains,
were gathered together and made one,
so may your Church be built up from the ends of the
    earth
and gathered into your kingdom. (Didache:9)

14. LIFE-GIVING FOOD

Heavenly Father,
your Son is the food that nourishes the whole world
giving life in abundance to all people.
May this bread,
broken that we may deepen our union with you
and our neighbor,
be the sign of your continual blessing.

15. BREAD FROM HEAVEN

Our Father gives us the bread from heaven
and the saving cup brimming with life.
May this bread broken and cup poured
link us together in charity and peace
so that we may be living signs of the Lord's kingdom.

16. COMMUNITY

As we share this bread,
we proclaim our willingness
to build a community of love,
to be the holy people
that God calls us to be.

17. ONE YET MANY

It takes many grains of wheat to make this bread.
It is one yet many.
To live as a community
we must be one though many.
And so in the breaking and sharing
we recognize the presence of the Lord Jesus
making us one.

18.   TRUE BREAD

Jesus is the true bread come down from heaven.
He blesses our earth.
He is the bread of life,
now broken into many pieces
to give us nourishment
and to be a constant reminder
that in the eating of this one bread,
we proclaim we are brothers and sisters of the same
    Father.

19.   EMMAUS

When Jesus was at table with them,
he took the bread and blessed and broke it,
and gave it to them.

And their eyes were opened
and they recognized him
in the breaking of the bread. (Luke 24:30-31)

20.   I AM

I am the resurrection and the life. (John 11:25)
I am the light of the world. (John 8:12)
I am the way, the truth, and the life. (John 14:6)
I am the vine, you are the branches. (John 15:5)
I am the bread of life. (John 6:35)

21. BREAD AND WINE

Through your Word, Father,
earth reflects your goodness.
Grains and vines sprout forth to nourish your people.
May this blessed bread, now broken for all,
be a symbol of your love
and a reminder of the charity
that we are called to share with one another.

Like the grapes that have been pressed into this holy
     wine,
press us together in your love and understanding.

B. LONGER FRACTION RITES

22. ETERNAL LIFE

The bread that sustains our life is Christ.
He is the food that assures our salvation.
"I myself am the living bread come down from
    heaven.
If anyone eats of this bread of mine, he shall live
    forever." (John 6:51)

In the eating of this blessed bread,
broken for all,
old and young, rich and poor,
there is eternal life.
Welcome to his table.

23. GATHER YOUR PEOPLE

Cel.
We give you thanks, heavenly Father,
for the life and knowledge
you have revealed to us
through Jesus your Son.

Lec.
As this broken bread
was once scattered on the hillsides,
and being harvested together became one,
so gather your Church together
from the ends of the earth into your kingdom.
(Didache: 9)

24. THE EARLY CHURCH

And the company of those who believed
were of one heart and mind
and they devoted themselves to the apostles'
    teaching,
and fellowship, and to the breaking of bread and
    prayer.

And all who believed were together
and held all things in common;
and they sold their possessions
and distributed them as any had need.

And day by day,
attending the temple together
and breaking bread in their homes,
they partook of food with glad and generous hearts.
(Acts 2:44-46)

25.   BREAD PASSED, CUP SHARED

We break bread
so that by sharing this meal
we meet Christ our Lord.
In him dawns a new age of unity with the Father.
In him peoples of all nations will sit down at table
as brothers and sisters in the kingdom of God.

In the silence of our faith,
Christ speaks to us of the hidden joys of life.
May this cup, passed in his fellowship,
be a sign of the kingdom hidden in our hearts.
May it keep us aware of your presence in all men and
    women.

26. DIDACHE: 10

Heavenly Father,
 you did create all things for your name's sake,
 and give food and drink to us for enjoyment
 that we might render thanks to you.
 You bestow upon us
 spiritual food and drink and eternal life through your
    Son.

Before all things we give you thanks
 that you are powerful;
 yours is the glory for ever and ever.
 Remember, Lord, your Church;
 perfect it in your love;
 and gather it together from the four winds
 into your kingdom which you have prepared for it,
 for yours is the power and the glory for ever and
    ever.

27. MAY THEY BE ONE

Cel.
As we break this bread
in memory of our Lord Jesus Christ,
we call to mind his prayer for all of us:

Lec.
I do not pray for these only,
but also for those
who believe in me through their word,
that they may all be one;
even as you, Father, are in me, and I in you,
that they also may be in us
so that the world may believe that you sent me.
The glory which you have given me
I have given to them,
that they may be one even as we are one,
I in them and you in me,
that they may become perfectly one
so that the world may know that you have sent me
and have loved them even as you have loved me.
(John 17:20-23)

Cel.
May our breaking of this bread of life
and our sharing of this meal
bring us together and make us one,
to the glory of God the Father.

28. JUSTIN MARTYR

We call this food the eucharist
of which no one may partake
except he who believes the truth of our teachings
and who has been washed for the forgiveness of sins
and for his regeneration,
and who lives as Christ has directed.

For we do not receive this bread and wine
as ordinary food or ordinary drink,
but rather,
just as through the Father's word
did our Savior Jesus Christ become incarnate
and took upon himself both flesh and blood
for our salvation,
so, we have been taught,
the food which has been made the eucharist
by the prayer of his word
is both the flesh and blood
of that Jesus who was made flesh.

This is truly the body and blood of our Lord Jesus
      Christ.
Let us remember that as often as we eat this bread
and drink this cup,
we proclaim the death of the Lord
until he comes in glory. (I Cor. 11:26)

29. JOHN 6:27-35

Cel.
"Do not labor for the food which perishes,
but for the food which endures to eternal life,
which the Son of man will give to you;
for on him has God the Father set his seal."

Lec.
Then they said to him,
"What must we do, to be doing the works of God?"

Cel.
Jesus answered them,
"This is the work of God,
that you believe in him whom he has sent."

Lec.
"Then what sign do you do,
that we may see and believe you?
What work do you perform?
Our fathers ate the manna in the wilderness;
as it is written,
'He gave them bread from heaven to eat.' "

Cel.
"Truly, truly, I say to you,
it was not Moses who gave you the bread from
        heaven;
my Father gives you the true bread from heaven.

For the bread of God
is that which comes down from heaven,
and gives life to the world."

Lec.
"Lord, give us this bread always."

Cel.
"I am the bread of life;
he who comes to me shall not hunger,
and he who believes in me shall never thirst."

30. BROKEN, CRUSHED, AND FILLED

Cel.
Father, we break bread,
once again remembering the night
when your Son passed from pain into your loving
    hands.
Your Son was broken and crushed,
but you filled him with glory.
He sent us his Spirit to be the undying fire
that bids us eat and drink in peace and brotherhood.

Cong.
When we eat this bread and drink this cup,
we proclaim your death, Lord Jesus,
until you come in glory. (I Cor. 11:26)

Cel.
This cup which is one,
is the sign of Christ's making.
Only crushed as grapes one for another,
can we live in him
and share his Spirit among us.
(Moser: *Home Celebrations*)

31. EZEKIEL

I myself will search for my sheep,
and will seek them out.
As a shepherd seeks out his flock
when some of his sheep have been scattered abroad,
so will I seek out my sheep;
and I will rescue them from all places
where they have been scattered
on a day of cloud and thick darkness.

I will feed them with good pasture,
and upon the mountain heights of Israel shall be their
    pasture;
there they shall lie down in good grazing land,
and on fat pasture they shall feed on the mountains
    of Israel.
I myself will be the shepherd of my sheep,
and I will make them lie down, says the Lord God.
I will seek the lost,
and I will bring back the strayed,
and I will bind up the crippled,
and I will strengthen the weak,
and I will feed them in justice.

I will make them
and the places round about my hill a blessing;
and I will send down the showers in their season;
they shall be showers of blessing.
And the trees of the field shall yield their fruit,
and the earth shall yield its increase,
and they shall be secure in their land;
and they shall know that I am the Lord. (Ezekiel: 34)

32. BODY AND BLOOD

Father, we ask that in the breaking of this bread
our eyes may be opened
so that we may recognize the presence of your Son
        among us.

The bread which we break,
is it not communion in the body of Christ?

And the cup of blessing which we bless,
is it not communion in the blood of Christ?
(I Cor. 10:16)

This is the bread which came down from heaven;
he who eats this bread will live forever.
(John 6:50-51)

This is truly the body and blood of our Lord Jesus
        Christ.
Let us remember that as often as we eat this bread
        and drink
this cup we proclaim the death of the Lord until he
        comes. (I Cor. 11:26)

Come now and receive the body and blood of Christ.

33. OUR DAILY BREAD

This fraction prayer accompanies the thanksgiving prayer,
Mercy.

Deacon
This bread which we break
is the new manna in the desert.
Though death stalk us like a lion
or despair like a wolf,
still this bread of life
will be ours to bless, break, and share.
Let us now pray to the Father:
Give us this day our daily bread.

Cong.
Give us this day our daily bread.

Deacon
When we are led into the desert,
and our spirits wither like grass . . .

Cong.
Give us this day our daily bread.

Deacon
When the fire of love dies down in us,
and ashes threaten to choke our souls . . .

Cong.
Give us this day our daily bread.

Deacon
When we forget your promise, Lord,
and our hope vanishes like smoke . . .

Cong.
Give us this day our daily bread.

Deacon
When we taste the ashes of sorrow
and forget the bread of life . . .

Cong.
Give us this day our daily bread.

Deacon
When we are tempted to turn our faces
and look away from our brothers and sisters in
     need . . .

Cong.
Give us this day our daily bread.

Deacon
When we drift from this table of fellowship
and starve in the desert of selfishness . . .

Cong.
Give us this day our daily bread.

34. MARANATHA

Cel.
Now let us break the bread of life
in a sharing of communion
and community in the Lord.
As we break bread together
we remember the Revelation of John
and the words of the Lord to us:
"Here I stand knocking at the door;
if anyone hears my voice and opens the door,
I will come in and sit down to supper with him,
and he with me." (Rev. 3:20)

Let us share this meal with hearts unlocked,
remembering the words of Jesus:
"I shall indeed be with you soon." (Rev. 22:7)
And let us answer: "Amen. Come, Lord Jesus!"
(I Cor. 16:22)

Cong.
Amen. Come, Lord Jesus!

35. PARTICIPATION

We partake of this bread, heavenly Father,
as a sign of our unity;
for what seems unliving,
is charged with the life of your Son.

This is the wine of the promised land
where the Lord sits at dinner with his children:
where they join hands around his table
and lay open their arms and hearts to one another
in Spirit and in truth. (Moser: *Home Celebrations*)

36. JOHN

I am the bread of life.
Your fathers ate the manna in the wilderness
and they died.
This is the bread which comes down from heaven,
that a man may eat of it and not die.
(John 6:48-50)

I am the living bread
which came down from heaven;
if anyone eats of this bread, he will live for ever;
and the bread which I shall give
for the life of the world is my flesh.
(John 6:51)

He who eats my flesh
and drinks my blood has eternal life,
and I will raise him up at the last day.
For my flesh is food indeed,
and my blood is drink indeed.
(John 6:54-56)

37. FELLOWSHIP

As the Holy Spirit strengthens your Church,
may this, your blessed bread,
which is now broken bring life to us.
May we be living signs of the charity
we share with one another.

May this, your holy cup,
poured out for all, be our salvation.
We pray that we who drink from the one cup
may be faithful signs of your love.

38. DIDACHE: 9,10

Cel.

(holding the cup)
We give you thanks, heavenly Father,
for the holy vine of your son, David,
which you have made known to us
through your Son Jesus.

Cong.
Yours is the glory for ever and ever.

Cel.

(holding the broken bread)
We give you thanks, heavenly Father,
for the life and knowledge
which you have made known to us
through your Son Jesus.

Cong.
Yours is the glory for ever and ever.

Cel.

As this broken bread
was scattered upon the mountains
and being gathered together became one,
so may your Church be gathered together
from the ends of the earth into your kingdom.

Cong.
For yours is the glory and the power
through Jesus Christ
for ever and ever.

39. BANQUET

Lec.
Isaiah proclaims:
"On this mountain,
God will prepare a banquet.
The finest food and best wine
will be served for all to partake.
On that day it will be said:
Behold, this is our God,
in him we hope for salvation." (Isaiah 25:6,9)
Confident in the Lord, we can sing (say):

Cong.
When we eat this bread and drink this cup
we proclaim the death of the Lord
until he comes in glory. (I Cor. 11:26)

Lec.
Jesus said,
"Truly, I say to you,
not even in Israel have I found such faith.
I tell you, many will come from east and west
and sit at table with Abraham, Isaac, and Jacob
in the kingdom of heaven." (Matthew 8:10-11)
Confident in the promise of Christ we can sing (say):

Cong.
Refrain.

Lec.
"You are those
who have continued with me in my trials;
as my Father appointed a kingdom for me,
so do I appoint for you
that you may eat and drink at my table
in my kingdom." (Luke 22:28-30)
Confident in the promise of Christ, we can sing (say):

Cong.
Refrain.

Lec.
The Apocalypse sees the kingdom fulfilled as a
        banquet:
"Write this: Blessed are those
who are invited to the marriage supper of the
        Lamb." (Rev. 19:9)
Filled with confidence, we can joyfully proclaim:

Cong.
Refrain.

Cel.
(holding the bread and wine)
This is the supper of the Lamb of God.
Broken that we might be whole,
the Lord Jesus shared himself
that we might live together
in the peace of God's children.
(Moser, *Home Celebrations*)

Happy are we who are called to his supper.

Cong.
Lord, I am not worthy to receive you,
but only say the word and I shall be healed.

40. LOAVES

Lec.
Jesus said,
"Make the people sit down."
In number about five thousand sat down.
Jesus then took the loaves,
and when he had given thanks,
he distributed them to those who were seated;
so also the fish, as much as they wanted.
When the people saw the sign
which he had done, they said:
"This is indeed the prophet
who is to come into the world!"
(John 6:10-12,14)

Cel.
This is the bread of life and the cup of salvation.
"He who comes to me shall not hunger,
and he who believes in me shall never thirst."
(John 6:35)

41. AUGUSTINE

The Lord left us in this sacrament
his body and blood.
Now we are called to become his body,
and through his mercy we are what we receive.

Just as you see that the bread is one loaf,
so may you be one body by loving one another,
by having one faith, one hope, and undivided charity.

Thus too, the wine existed in many clusters of grapes
and now it is one.
It is one in this cup after the crushing
of the grapes in the wine press.

And now, you, in the name of Christ,
have come to drink of the cup of the Lord.
There you are on the table,
and there you are in the cup,
for you are one with us.
We receive together,
and we drink together
because we live together.

42. IGNATIUS OF ANTIOCH

Come together in common,
one and all without exception in charity,
in one faith and in one Jesus Christ,
the Son of God and Son of man,
so that with undivided mind
you may break one bread
which is the medicine of immortality
and the remedy against death,
enabling us to live for ever in Jesus Christ.

43. WE BECOME WHAT WE RECEIVE

The bread which you see on the table
is the body of Christ.
What the cup holds is
the blood of Christ
poured out for us and for all men
that sins might be forgiven.

May we become what we receive.
As Paul the Apostle says:
The bread is one;
we though many, are one body.
(St. Augustine)

May we learn this lesson from the bread of life
and cherish unity now and always.

44. JOHN CHRYSOSTOM

God gave one house for all of us to dwell in.
It is called the world.
God distributed all created things equally.
He kindled one sun for all;
stretched above us one roof, the sky;
and set up one table, which is the earth.

But God also gave us a much greater table than this.
It is the table of one loaf and one cup.
We have been made rich
and one in this bread and wine.

Then, whence comes the great inequality
of conditions in life?
From greed and arrogance.

But let this be no longer.
Since we are made one in this meal,
let us not be driven asunder
by envy, greed, jealousy and hatred.
All these are grand illusions for those
who partake of the meal of eternal life.

May this meal we share
preserve this unity unbroken.

45. THE MARK OF A CHRISTIAN

Cel.
What is the mark of a Christian?

Cong.
That we be holy and blameless
and so eat the body of Christ
and drink his blood.

Cel.
And what is the mark of those
who eat the bread
and drink the cup of Christ?

Cong.
That they keep in perpetual remembrance
him who died for us and rose again.

Cel.
What is the mark
of those who keep such remembrance?

Cong.
That they live not for themselves
but for him who died for us and rose again.

Cel.
What, then, is the mark of a Christian?

Cong.

That our justice abound in all things
more than that of the scribes and the Pharisees,
according to the Lord's gospel.

Cel.

What is the mark of a Christian?

Cong.

To set the Lord always in our sight,
to watch daily and hourly
and to stand prepared in that state
knowing that the Lord comes
when we least expect him.

Cel.

So, then, what is the mark of a Christian?

Cong.

That we love one another
as Christ loves us.
(St. Basil)